Who says you can't

CHANGE THE WORLD?

Jubilee Campaign: challenging injustice

Who says you can't
CHANGE THE WORLD?

Jubilee Campaign: challenging injustice

Danny Smith

First published 2003 by Spring Harvest Publishing Division
and Authentic Lifestyle

09 08 07 06 05 04 03   7 6 5 4 3 2 1

Authentic Lifestyle is an imprint of Authentic Media
PO Box 300, Carlisle, Cumbria CA3 0QS
and PO Box 1047, Waynesboro, GA 30830-2047, USA
www.paternoster-publishing.com

British Library Cataloguing in Publication Data

A catalogue record for this book is available from the British
Library

1-85078-517-1

Some names have been changed for reasons of
security or sensitivity

Cover design by Darren Southworth S2 Design
Printed in Great Britain by Bell & Bain Ltd., Glasgow

Contents

Evil triumphs when good people remain silent
and do nothing.
(with acknowledgement to Edmund Burke)

Danny's book will keep you enthralled – I couldn't put it down as I raced with him through continents and countries with tenterhooks, traumas and tears. What can be done with God to set the captives free, alleviate suffering and turn tragedy into triumph is presented here with a driving energy for justice. Thank you, Danny, for not only a good read, but also a challenging, inspiring and faith-expanding look into your life.

ROGER FORSTER Leader Ichthus Christian Fellowship:
Honorary vice-president of the
Evangelical Alliance and of Tearfund

I was riveted from the first page of this powerful book and couldn't stop reading it. This is an amazing account of people at risk in countries around the world and the determined fight of a few 'sold out' people who willingly risked their lives to bring justice to the perpetrators of such appalling abuse.

FIONA CASTLE

Danny Smith has been at the forefront of many human rights battles, most of which are included in this book. With its gripping narrative, *Who says you can't change the world?* is a passionate plea for Christians to get involved: to protect the vulnerable and fight for the safety and well-being of children and others around the world. I enthusiastically recommend it to you.

STEVE CHALKE, Founding Director, Oasis Trust

Reading Danny Smith, you need to remind yourself at the turn of every page, this is not some adventure yarn laced with death threats, kidnap and car chases to enthral. This is a price paid daily by those trying to protect the children nobody wants. In a disturbing account, he touches the darkness of the soul, showing us how governments condone the murder of their children or their use by sex tourists. Danny Smith doesn't preach, but has a talent to amuse and enlighten, though at the end of this book I guarantee you will feel shame for not doing more to support the quiet heroism of such men. What this book proves is that if you care enough, and you make the effort, you can make a difference. Indeed, if it weren't for the likes of him, you would wonder if it isn't time for the species to move over and give the apes a crack at running the planet.

DANIEL McGRORY
Award winning journalist, The Times

This highly readable book provides a moving account of many of the achievements of the Jubilee story. It shows how a small and dedicated group can make an incalculable difference for some of the most vulnerable and oppressed people in the world. Danny Smith writes in a way which makes it impossible to put the book down: compelling, exciting, moving and inspiring. I recommend this book wholeheartedly as a source of inspiration and challenge.

THE BARONESS COX

Every revolution has its heroes. Often the most effective agents are not the ones that ride the movement to fame or notoriety. Over recent decades a revolution has occurred and Danny Smith has been and is a driving force behind the drama of change. *Who says you can't change the world?* is much more than a book of high-risk, exciting adventures. It is the account of a visionary who, driven by a clear inner conviction, would put his life on the line again and again for the sake of the poor and defenceless. That is a Jesus life-style.

LYNN GREEN Youth With A Mission

Danny Smith's *Who says you can't change the world?* is a deeply thought-provoking and incisive book, looking into one of the most hateful and destructive evils that man can render to man: the abuse of innocent children. The message of Jubilee Campaign is truly to be an instrument of justice and peace, working towards a world where the vision of St Francis, the poor man of Assisi, is fulfilled: where all created things live in harmony and are equal.

FATHER MICHAEL SEED SA
Franciscan friar and worker for Christian Unity,
Westminster Cathedral

I found it hard to put down – I was right there on the streets, in the rubbish tip, walking through the red light districts and in the cramped prison rooms – my heart skipping beats! Thank God for people like Danny, who do what I know I couldn't do myself.

CINDY KENT Premier Radio

Gripping stuff!

DOMINIC SMART,
Senior Minister Gilcomston South Church,
Aberdeen

Danny speaks with the authority of one who has lived and worked in the trenches of this modern day 'Dickensian' travesty. His integrity and authenticity is unquestionable, his heart and compassion a challenge to all.

PHIL WALL, Hope 10/10

Life is a great adventure with many uncertainties and surprises. It's certainly been that for Danny Smith of the Jubilee Campaign. This is a remarkable story of their fight for justice and a reminder to us all that each of us can make a difference. *Who says you can't change the world?* is an excellent book.

MATT BIRD Director, Joshua Generation

Under Danny Smith's inspired leadership, the Jubilee Campaign's work for the persecuted church has ensured that the cry of the voiceless been heard not just in the corridors of power at Westminster, but in worldwide forums such as the US Congress and the United Nations. This book's story of the perseverance of the Campaign in the face of tall odds is an inspiration to others to take on some of the huge challenges of world poverty and injustice. It will be welcomed by all to ensure the marginalised are not forgotten.

RAM GIDOOMAL CBE
Leader, Christian Peoples Alliance

This exciting and dramatic story re-lives some of the incredible campaigns that Danny and his Jubilee team have been involved in. In a world riddled with hate and violence, this book about truth and justice will encourage you to want to serve others - whatever the cost.

DAN WOODING
Founder ASSIST News Service

Who says you can't change the world? is an exciting read. Danny's journalistic style captures the excitement of days in which evangelical Christians returned to their roots. Campaigns for religious liberty, working on behalf of the oppressed, and seeing the release of the persecuted are all part of our evangelical heritage. It's wonderful to relive the thrill of watching God use His people to work on behalf of those who had endured much for their faith and thoroughly deserved their freedom!

Clive Calver, President, World Relief

Foreword

Children at the school I attended were encouraged to write two Latin words at the head of each piece of work: *Auctore Deo* – the enterprise is of God. The extended thought is, of course, that if the enterprise is not of God then it is doomed to fail. As I write this introduction, I want to put those words at the head and heart of this text. I do not believe that Jubilee would have flourished without God's blessing. Three steps: see, evaluate, act, have always been present in Jubilee's mission. First is the necessity of seeing what the world often chooses not to see. Then, in arriving at an evaluation there needs to be a careful assimilation and assessment of the facts. Finally, there is the requirement to act.

Initially, Jubilee's work centred on the persecution of Christians in the former Soviet Union. So often their suffering had been overlooked. In the west we chose not to see. Canon Michael Bordeaux, the inspirational founder of Keston College, who monitored the plight of the suffering church, described how it was politically convenient for church leaders and parliamentarians to hide behind the excuse that 'intervening will only make their situation worse.' This was not the wish of many Christians – Orthodox, Protestant and Catholic – and, in the wake of the successful campaign to free the Seven Siberian Christians who had been holed up in the basement of the American Embassy in Moscow, Jubilee was determined that the world should see and understand the fate of their co-religionists on the other side of the Iron Curtain.

With Danny Smith's encouragement and vision, Jubilee Campaign has engaged with regimes of every ilk, in championing the rights of people suffering for their religious beliefs. Primarily this has focused on Christians but not exclusively. Among the Karen, for instance, there are also Buddhists, Muslims, and people of traditional faiths, who have been persecuted too.

Perhaps one of Jubilee's greatest strengths has been that in its inception we drew heavily on both the evangelical and Catholic traditions. Almost all Christian traditions have been represented in Jubilee's work

Danny Smith and Lord Alton on their way to lobby the South African Ambassador over detainees, 1988.

Photo: Kevin Hutson

– those we have campaigned for and those who have campaigned for them.

Out of the work for the persecuted church came Jubilee Action. Having seen the plight of children in many parts of the world, Danny wanted us to take the same three steps of seeing, evaluating and acting, on their behalf. When we look at seemingly intractable world problems, we could so easily be tempted into believing that there is nothing we can do. When James Mawdsley went to Burma, he was thrown into prison, given a seventeen year prison sentence and spent thirteen months in solitary confinement. Jubilee gave his supporters small stones to carry. Each stone represented the duty of each of us to carry one another's burden. It was a reminder to take the double action of pressure and prayer. But the small stone also reminds us that landslides happen when small stones move – and that is what we are, the small stones. Jubilee hired a boat to take some of James' supporters past Westminster on the first anniversary of his imprisonment. We heard from human rights activists and from Karen speakers. There was political pressure and prayer. As the boat turned to make its way back up the Thames, there was a moored dredging barge close to the bank. On an awning were the words 'Landslides, no problem.'

Perhaps, as Jubilee's work goes forward we should see ourselves as the small stones working for the landslides and recognise that if the enterprise truly is of God then none of these great challenges is insuperable. That Jubilee has come so far is a great testimony to the persistence and vision of Danny Smith. None of us who met in Westminster's Jubilee Room, all those years ago, had any idea of what was being launched or how it would grow. Yet its achievements have been significant.

Lord Alton of Liverpool

Introduction

A Car Park in Epsom...1995

It was late in the evening and Epsom's multi-storey car park was deserted. We drove in a convoy up to the third level and pulled over in one of the empty bays. Fast Eddie was the first out and walked over, carrying a heavy silver case.

'OK, this is it,' he said. 'Take off your clothes.'

I shrugged, took off my shirt, pulled down my trousers. Goose bumps came up on my body as the cool evening breeze hit hard.

The squeal of tyres startled us. A black Golf GTi came into view. It hit the curve of the exit route and cruised by. We froze for an instant and must have had the collective look of a fawn caught in the brights of a car's main beam. The driver of the Golf seemed to be a prim, no-nonsense, career woman. You could read her quizzical expression as she took in the scene, setting her mental clock to be sure to catch *Crimewatch* the following Tuesday. 'Yes, officer, there were six of them. They looked really mean. One was stripped, almost naked.'

'Come on guys, let's get to work.' It was Fast Eddie and in the next twenty minutes, we realised how he had earned his nickname.

Fast Eddie pulled open the silver case to reveal a cascade of electronic gadgetry. His blonde assistant, Jade, strapped a mini-tape recorder to my lower chest and a sound box to my side. I pulled on my shirt and a loose-fitting jacket that I had bought for £1 from Oxfam earlier that day. They traced the wires through my clothes and plugged me in. Jade checked sound levels. At first, it was hard to breathe with the multi-flex heavy-duty tape cutting into my skin and the equipment strapped so tightly to my body. Adam Chadwick, who was in charge of the operation, pointed to my reflection in the car mirror. 'You've put on a lot of weight,' he smirked.

Meanwhile Fast Eddie was putting the final touches to the last hi-tech gizmo from his bag of tricks. It was a necktie. Attached to it were wires linked to a sleek-looking box with flashing lights. He carefully eased the tie over my head and placed it around my neck. Jade traced the cable through my shirt and plugged it into the sound box taped to my waist.

'OK, we're live,' Fast Eddie announced. He twiddled with some buttons and static burst out from the sound box. 'Let's hit it.'

With deft, precise strokes, they wired me for sound and pictures. A low light flicked from the small television monitor that Jade was holding and Adam's image appeared on the screen. Adam stood in front of me and waved. And there he was on the monitor. Waving. But where was the image coming from? Jade pointed to my necktie.

The tie wasn't going to win any design awards. Little diamond-shaped motifs the size of a small button were set tight against a lazy silvery silk material. At the centre of the pattern of one of the diamond shapes was a tiny camera lens.

Fast Eddie's work was immaculate. The camera was virtually undetectable and the floppy coat covered the recorders taped to my body. He was in constant demand by television reporters and had worked on many under-cover investigations for Roger Cook and others. Adam had chosen this particular day for this operation because he wanted Fast Eddie for the job. He told me, 'It's going to be dangerous and I want to be sure we have the best.'

'You know what you have to do, don't you?' Fast Eddie said, talking me through the best positions to capture the target on the secret camera.

Some months earlier, ITV's *News at Ten* wrote and asked if they could work with us on an undercover operation that we had started, to investigate travel agents in the UK who were selling 'child sex' tours overseas. Jubilee Campaign had been at the forefront of a campaign to identify sex tourists who abused children around the world and to seek changes in the law so that they could be prosecuted here in the UK. Under existing legislation, men could videotape themselves violating children overseas but if they were caught at Heathrow Airport, they could only be prosecuted for carrying obscene videos. The sex acts against children were not punishable. It was absurd.

When we approached the government to introduce laws to prosecute such sex tourists, they expressed their sympathy but performed the ceremony of the folded arms. They would do everything they could but there was nothing they could do. Britain once led the world in ending the slave trade but by 1995 remained the only major tourist-sending country to refuse to introduce a law prosecuting Britons participating in the enslavement of children overseas.

The government's feeble excuses effectively left them on the side of the sex tourists. It was hard to understand why more was not being done to protect children at risk. How could we allow children around the world to be enslaved and held captive for adults to jet in and defile them? How would history judge us? We had to give everything we had, including ourselves, to fight this evil. There was no option.

We were sure that the fast track to the government's attention was to get the story into the press. When our partner in the Philippines, Father Shay Cullen, video-taped the arrest of a suspected paedophile – a foreigner – on a boat with young children (some aged seven) I was sure that the story would cause a sensation. After screening the video, the media groups we approached were enthusiastic but when they learned that the perpetrator, Victor Fitzgerald, was Australian and not British, the decision was swift and emphatic. The offender had to be British or the story wouldn't run.

Together with Father Shay in the Philippines we launched our own investigation into the dark, sordid, claustrophobic world of sex tourists. Several leads emerged. With the backing of ITV, we knew the story had legs.

One of our targets, Michael Stone, the boss of a Surrey travel agency called 747 Travel, talked enthusiastically about the sex industry abroad and promised personally to escort me around the bars and brothels of Thailand and the Philippines – after I had purchased a ticket from him.

'We can get you anything you want,' Stone said convincingly, 'including young girls.'

'But just how young are they?' I asked.

He replied, 'Just tell me how young you want the girls. Just give me an age. Just give me a number. No problem at all. You can do anything you want with the kids.'

Stone wanted a cheque in the post for my ticket but I was insistent that we met and the lure of my payment proved too enticing. I had tape-recorded several telephone conversations with him but for the story to run on television, he had to repeat his statements to me in person.

The risks were obvious. If Stone sensed that he had been exposed, he'd erupt in fury. If he suspected that I was filming him …

When the ITV news team learned that he worked from home and sold his sex tours within a mile of Chessington's World of Adventures, they had the hook for an important story.

I had always wanted to be an actor but playing the role of a suspected paedophile soliciting children for sex was one of the toughest things I've had to do. I would give my life for my children, now safe at home, given all the love and care that our hearts could afford. But here I was, late at night, in leafy, tranquil Surrey, with a sleaze bag whose job involved selling tickets to perverts so they could travel and then abuse and torture children.

From the car park in Epsom we drove the short journey to 747 Travel, situated in an elegant suburb near Epsom. The film crew set up their equipment in the bushes at the side of the road and focused their camera on Stone's front door.

I walked down the quiet avenue and pressed the door bell. I was sweating slightly, both from nervous tension and the equipment strapped to my body. The tape cut into my flesh and the decks and the wires under my clothes were uncomfortable.

Curiously, I felt a sense of calm, despite the obvious anxiety.

Somewhere to the left, I caught a glimpse of a woman being pulled along by a dog straining on its leash. In the distance, a car engine started up, followed quickly by the crackle crunch of tyres on gravel.

The door opened and I walked inside.

1

Throwaway Children

Jubilee Campaign has been described as a small family business with the impact and influence of a multinational corporation.

We had led several high profile campaigns, captured international media coverage and gained widespread support from politicians and personalities. The secret of a successful campaign was to combine a simple, clear, achievable objective with a strategic plan that could involve as many people as possible, and to sustain that energy and effort over a reasonable period of time.

A report by John Pilger in the *Daily Mirror* revealed how he had purchased a child in Thailand and it haunted me for years. I always wanted to respond but the issue of child prostitution was different. The problem was too big. We were too small. Nothing we could do would make any difference. What was the point of doing anything?

All that changed the day I met Father Shay Cullen, an Irish priest, from the Columban Missionary order.

While attending a mission conference in the Philippines in 1992, I dropped out of some sessions to talk to local agencies who were concerned with the problem of the commercial sex industry. Even a cursory glance confirmed that children were ensnared and, while most groups had 'projects', everyone directed me to an Irish priest as the leading authority on the issue.

Shay patrolled the jails and back streets of Olongapo City in the Philippines, once called the biggest brothel in the world. This was his parish. The street children and child prostitutes were his flock. His objective was to defend the rights of children and he tracked down suspected paedophiles with the combined dedication of an Old Testament prophet and a modern day detective.

Shay was practical and down to earth and we became close friends and partners. He had none of the false piety of some church leaders, but possessed all the practical spirituality of someone who knew what it was like to live in the city. He had witnessed great evil and was compelled to confront it, within the context of his faith and experience.

Throwaway children. Rosie, aged five years old, was rescued from prison in Olongapo City by Father Shay Cullen.   Photo: Father Shay Cullen

Shay explained his life's work in this way

I have a special mission to work for justice and peace and to bear witness to the truth. Part of my work is prophetic, that is to take a stand for justice. Christianity in action is solidarity with very poor people, with those who have been oppressed, like in Olongapo, taking a stand, and not being intimidated but following in the footsteps of Jesus. I'm not a moral crusader. I am fighting for justice. Justice is at the very heart of the message of Jesus. Working for justice is central to Christianity. Wherever justice is being done it is a sign that we love one another. I feel a righteous anger when I see injustice in the world – especially in the third world countries like the Philippines – where the rich grow richer on the sweat of the poor.

In the late sixties, Shay was assigned to the Philippines as a young parish priest. He worked with the urban poor, developing handicraft products that were sold to local American military personnel. For more than nine decades, the United States had retained a military presence amongst the 7,017 scattered islands that made up the Republic of the Philippines, with the biggest naval base outside America located at Olongapo City. The massive US air force squadron was situated at nearby Clark Field, Angeles City. With America at war in Vietnam, the islands of the Philippines were of strategic significance for the military and conveniently located for rest and recreation for their soldiers engaged in the conflict in South East Asia.

In 1983, a local nun came to the young Irish priest with a problem. Eighteen street girls, aged between nine to fourteen years, infected with venereal disease, were being treated at a sex clinic. The children told of being sold for sex to foreign customers who paid between $10 and $20 to use them. The nun had expressed her concern to the mayor of Olongapo City who told her to ignore the 'petty issue' and not to tell anyone. She disobeyed him and went directly to Shay.

One of the girls, a nine-year-old called Jennifer, was left bleeding. She used a T-shirt belonging to one of the navy officers to stop the blood. The T-shirt contained an important clue, revealing a navy laundry tag that could be used to find the offender. When the owner of the T-shirt was tracked down, Shay was genuinely shocked to discover two things: the US navy were reluctant to help and local politicians, benefiting from the US trade, pressured him to join the cover-up. Don't make waves, he was told.

Meanwhile the owner of the T-shirt slipped quietly out of Subic Bay.

Shay gave the US navy a deadline: if the culprit could not be found in a week, he would go public with the story. When seven days passed in stony silence, the story hit the headlines, and eventually the T-shirt was traced to US navy officer Daniel J. Dougherty. This forced the US navy to act. And they did. Dougherty was found guilty on thirteen counts of child abuse. But the offender faced a military court in Guam, not in the Philippines, and his punishment was to undergo psychiatric treatment for one year. There were many who shared Shay's feeling that Dougherty had got away lightly.

Shay had created a stir and there were consequences.

Overnight, the army stopped purchasing handicrafts from his centre and the work collapsed, but on the street, the word spread that this young Irish priest was the man to contact if you were in trouble in Olongapo City. Day or night. For Shay, it must have seemed as though he was seeing everything for the first time. Those familiar places where he walked and the people he saw were players in a dark, unfolding tragedy.

Olongapo City was home to about one hundred and twenty thousand people but without the US presence, it is unlikely that it would have been anything more than a quaint fishing village. The base employed about twenty-one thousand Filipinos while around five thousand US military and civilians and their families were stationed there permanently. Thousands more visited on ships and carriers and at the peak of the Vietnam War, about twenty thousand could visit in a two week period. The US government estimated that about $1 million a day was pumped into the local economy by the base's personnel, both Filipino and Americans. Each time an aircraft-carrier docked in the bay, another ten thousand sailors took to the streets of this wild town.

The military base was considered a huge natural resource. Olongapo didn't have a factory and there were no plans to build one. The city had only one thing to offer: its young girls and women, and frequently their children.

Under successive regimes, places such as Olongapo and Angeles became sexual supermarkets, catering to an international clientele. About a thousand bars, night clubs and massage parlours with names like Hot Lips, Top Gun and Men's Paradise Tavern started just a few hundred metres from the main gate of the naval base. It was evident that the American presence spawned a culture of prostitution and a profitable sex industry was allowed to flourish catering for American servicemen and international tourists. They were seen as untouchable, no matter what they did.

But Shay couldn't remain silent and consequently, 108 cases of sexual abuse were filed against American servicemen over the next few years. Fifteen cases involved children between four and sixteen years of age. Most of the cases were either resolved in favour of the servicemen or settled out of court. Local officials were reluctant to prosecute American citizens for fear of upsetting the US authorities and because prostitution benefited the local economy. The Americans weren't about to get involved, despite Shay's evidence.

- A retired US serviceman, Jimmy Ray Irwin, aged forty-five, raped a six year old girl but was never prosecuted. Officials claimed that the US navy had not been helpful in tracing him, although he received his monthly pension regularly from Olongapo's US naval base.
- Laurence Charles Vensaka was accused of abusing children, aged between eight and fourteen years. He was on legal hold inside the base but disappeared. He was never traced.
- The depravity appeared to have no limits. In one documented episode, an eighteen month old child was

Father Shay patrols the jails of Olongapo City.
Photo: Preda

found to have gonorrhoea. Her mother was living with three US sailors at the time.

Shay's one-man campaign exposed the impact that the sex industry had made, and the increasing exploitation of children. In a newspaper column for a leading daily, the *Philippine Inquirer*, he wrote

> My concern is that prostitution and the streets will be the only life a child may know. Many of the women working in brothels serving US military and foreigners were street children themselves. One was fourteen years old when she first sold her body, and for twenty years she continued to do so until she was no longer 'marketable'. She then sold the only possession she had, her eleven year old daughter.

In time, his work revitalised itself and the Preda Centre, established in 1973 as a preventative and curative service for drug users, expanded into a residential project for street children and victims of sexual abuse. It was set up in genuine partnership with talented Filipinos, Lex and Merle Hermoso, and came to be recognised as a pioneering work to defend children's rights.

Shay clashed repeatedly with corrupt local politicians and businessmen who depended on the bars and brothels frequented by servicemen and tourists for the economic survival of their city. Harassment and intimidation gave way to deportation orders and death threats; the very officials who should have been deporting the paedophiles were the ones trying to deport Shay.

Shay's major adversary was the mayor, Richard Gordon, a power baron who controlled the city and ran it as his personal fiefdom. Gordon was determined to preserve the structures that appeased the Americans and ensured that Olongapo served their interests. Keen to avoid bad publicity, he was enraged when Shay took up the case of eighteen children infected with gonorrhoea and forced the arrest of the US navy officer involved.

Shay considered Gordon as representative of a wider problem. He explained

> The lives of the poor in Third World countries are characterised by economic and political oppression. The distribution of material wealth is unjust. It's like a pyramid with the top two percent dominating the life of everyone else. The power elite sit at the very top of the pile making their money off the backs of the poor. This unjust system provides the structure for the creation of poverty. In the Philippines, one hundred families can control the entire wealth of sixty-five million people. When the political system provides that kind of structure, it results in a powerful evil force oppressing the people and it has to be confronted. What is the purpose of a government if it is just promoting an environment of corruption and oppression? The ordinary people suffer a great deal and we suffer along with them. So why not? That is part of our mission and our duty.

Shay alleged that Gordon was linked to the corruption and the sex industry and he was duly sued for libel by the mayor in their epic feud that has lasted decades. The mayor denied the allegations but was unable to dispute the physical presence of rejects from the commercial sex industry, waifs and strays and kids that Shay and others called 'throwaway children'.

Rosario Baluyot was one of the 'throwaway children' who became a tragic token of the sleaze that permeated the city. Rosario lived on Olongapo's busiest street, Magsaysay Drive. She was a street girl who sold sticks of gum to earn a few pesos, sleeping in drop-in centres or curled up in doorways. When a foreigner offered her eight hundred pesos to go to a hotel, she knew what to expect but it was too much to turn down. The tourist kicked her out the next morning but left the broken tip of a vibrator lodged deep inside her. She was found lying in agony, in the streets, by Sister Eva Palencia, who rushed the child to hospital, accompanied by Shay.

She subsequently bled to death and it was left to Sister Eva, Shay and Rosario's friends to arrange her pitiful funeral. She was buried on a hilltop overlooking the city. The headstone, paid for by Shay, read simply

Rest In Peace
Rosario Baluyot
Alone in life, alone in death, except those of us who cannot
forget the throwaway children.

Rosario was twelve years old.

Mayor Gordon and the business community felt that giving publicity to such incidents tarnished the image of the city and seemed pleased with the slow pace with which the police pursued the murder inquiry into Rosario's death. But pressure from Sister Eva and Shay drove the investigation forward. Word hit the streets that the suspect had been spotted in a bar in Manila and with relevant eyewitnesses, they forced the arrest of Henrick Ritter, a medical graduate from Graz in Austria, on holiday in Olongapo.

Behind locked doors, a complex web of intrigue and corruption threatened to influence the outcome of the trial. Rosario's grandmother had been paid fifteen thousand pesos by Ritter to withdraw the complaint and promised an additional bonus of five thousand pesos if the case was dismissed. The deal was struck in the office of Ritter's lawyer, Edmundo Legaspi, who handed over the money. The footprints led to the top city officials. Legaspi had acted as a temporary city mayor during an election when Richard Gordon was running for political office. But the formidable team of Sister Eva and Shay counselled Rosario's grandmother to speak the truth and in this way honour the memory of her granddaughter. She held her nerve and her original complaint was upheld in court. It was also revealed that while in prison awaiting trial, Ritter succeeded in bribing the guards to bring a child into his cell.

Ritter was convicted of Rosario's rape and murder and given a life sentence. His verdict sent shock waves throughout the country. For Shay and the community in Olongapo City, Ritter's verdict represented a major victory. Justice had prevailed. Things would change. But all was not as it seemed. Within two years, Ritter was released on a technicality and fled.

He had got away.

Dark Invader

The US military acted as though nothing had happened but behind the scenes they observed the whirlwind that Shay had created and in time organised their own internal inquiry. The US Navy Investigative Bureau conducted an undercover operation, revealing that children as young as six were being sold into prostitution with US sailors, and identified eight suspects as pimps.

This secret report was covered up and never published. It was only revealed years later when Shay obtained the documents through the Freedom of Information Act in the US and facsimile copies were reproduced in a report we published in 1992 when we launched our campaign in Parliament to fight child prostitution.

The American officials were probably preoccupied with their own difficulties with the growing clamour to remove the US bases. Finally, after nine decades in the Philippines, the American military had no option but to pull out when the Philippine Senate voted to reject renewing the formal agreement between both countries. Many of the locals were in denial, not believing that the bases were closing but most of the massive carriers of the US naval fleet had completed final manoeuvres and were already sailing for home on the long journey across the Pacific. The last American ship to leave the Philippines did so from a remote isolated dock on 23 November 1992. Not many were on the waterfront dock to wave goodbye. One man who was there was Father Shay Cullen. Shay and the coterie of human rights activists with him clearly felt that their protests had played a part in the US's decision and they were justified in celebrating their departure.

While the endemic poverty, exploitation and corruption of the Philippines couldn't all be blamed on the Americans, it was considered that their presence had contributed to the problems and, as they sailed away, they left behind a country in ruins. The fresh coat of paint on some buildings couldn't hide the economic crisis, disintegrating infrastructure and stench of corruption that permeated the political culture. The problems started at the top. The political system, tightly controlled by President Marcos, was clearly bolstered by the Americans who relied on him to provide stability in the region and conveniently overlooked his excesses. It would later be alleged that Marcos had hidden half his country's gross national product in private foreign bank accounts. Not to be outdone, his wife, Imelda, would be remembered for her shoe collection – a staggering 3,500 pairs.

And when the Americans left, they never looked back. If they had, they might have seen Asian kids with blond hair and blue eyes, huddled in doorways, hustling on the streets, trawling through dustbins behind the bars and clubs in the city that never slept. The kids could also be seen scavenging for food on the mountain of garbage piled up on the outskirts of the city. At night, some found their way back home, curled up in hovels in shanty towns, their mothers struggling to cope, while trying to remember the American servicemen who had shared their life for passing moments and transitory pleasures.

These 'Amerasian' children, as they came to be known, were children of mixed parentage (an Asian mother and an American father). The term 'Amerasian' dated back to the Korean War in the early 1950s but came into popular usage during the Vietnam war, when the prolonged presence of American servicemen in South East Asia resulted in an increased number of such children. It was estimated that at the end of the Vietnam War, there were more than one hundred and twenty-five thousand Amerasian children left behind in Vietnam, while still others were born in neighbouring countries like Thailand, Laos, Cambodia, Korea, Japan, and, of course, the Philippines.

While the Amerasian children of Vietnam were eventually acknowledged, years later, the children of American and Filipino parents were constantly denied their birthright and child support – and this was only granted after lobbying by activists, including Shay. He filed a class action lawsuit against the US Navy in Washington DC, but the controversial case was dismissed on a technicality: the judge ruled that prostitution was illegal and therefore the court couldn't rule on an illegal act. Determined to pursue the case, Shay enlisted the support of US Congresswoman, Anne Eshoo, and a resolution was passed encouraging a grant of $2 million dollars to help the children. This was whittled down to $650,000 and distributed through the Pearl Buck Foundation, though what impact this really made is debatable.

Meanwhile, in Olongapo, the owners of the bars and massage parlours pumped up the music, turned on the neon signs and pushed their clutch of girls into the streets, pretending that nothing had happened. Business as usual. But the US servicemen were the engine driving the prostitution business and without their custom, the clubs and massage parlours were no longer the thriving enterprise that had given the city its sordid reputation.

Olongapo had virtually no other businesses or industry to sustain itself and without American servicemen on the prowl, many of the dance clubs and bars were forced to close their doors. It was estimated that there were about sixteen thousand women and children engaged in the sex business in Olongapo City, before the Americans left town, and the same number in nearby Angeles City, where the Clark base was located. And with the bases gone, many of the women and young girls who had turned to prostitution to survive found themselves destitute.

The cronies of the Gordon clan regrouped, determined to maintain the ruthless political machine and to remain in control of the city after the US departure. With curious predictability, Kate Gordon replaced her husband Richard as the new mayor and wangled a six year appointment for him to an influential position as the head of the newly formed Subic Bay Metropolitan Authority. This significant and lucrative job was given the nod by President Ramos, and six years later Gordon was again reconfirmed as Ramos stepped down. Cynical observers noted that the post was a reward for Gordon pulling out of the presidential race and backing Ramos' appointee – Senator Jose de Venecia. Power was consolidated within the Gordon oligarchy but when Joseph Estrada won the elections, in

1992, his first presidential decree was to get rid of Gordon, who fought back but lost.

While Gordon had ruled Olongapo City as mayor, the sex industry had developed into a thriving business. With the US bases empty, he encouraged foreigners in the area and tolerated, perhaps appeased, any deviancy in their behaviour. As a result, a motley group of ex-servicemen, drifters and exiles bought villas and clubs and took up residence. They liked the easy, free-wheeling life style, the tropical breezes of the sunny islands and the pleasant, friendly temperament of the locals. At night, they wandered back to their old haunts and the clubs and bars opened their doors once again. New girls were enticed into the business with the promise of easy money. Word spread that the old timers were back, trying to relive and reclaim the wild old days.

And with them came a dark, deviant invader.

Like conquistadors and adventurers of old, explorers mapping the new frontier, these modern prospectors weren't looking for unconquered lands, treasure or secret cities of gold. They came seeking children.

Man on the Run

Pagsangan was one of the Philippines' most popular resorts, with an abundance of natural hot springs, striking views, and a spectacular 300 foot waterfall, accessible by taking an hour long ride by dug-out canoe through a beautiful canyon. It was the splendour of these surroundings that attracted Francis Ford Coppola to choose Pagsangan to film *Apocalypse Now*, an epic film, starring Marlon Brando and Martin Sheen and loosely based on Joseph Conrad's novel *Heart of Darkness*.

An extra in Coppola's film was a flamboyant character called Andrew Mark Harvey. He had a bigger role in the Chuck Norris action blockbuster, *Missing in Action – Part III*, in which he played the part of a priest who helped the star to rescue some children and died heroically in the end.

Harvey was well known in the area for his affection for little boys and chose several of them to live with him in a lodge that he had set up amidst a particularly lovely spot in Pagsangan. He ingratiated himself with local families, many of whom were grateful for his handouts and his paying for their children's educational fees. Harvey introduced the boys to his friends, who descended on the lodge from around the world. They were impressed with the beautiful location and the willingness of the youths, who would do anything to please. His network was widespread and influential.

Harvey's life style was an open secret and the locals grew dependent on his favours. In return, they were willing to sacrifice their children. But there was a growing clamour to curb such activities, and Harvey was unexpectedly arrested and imprisoned at the Bureau of Immigration in Manila. Instead of being brought to trial for his crimes, the authorities inexplicably deported him, and he flew back to the US.

After his deportation, local activists arrived at Harvey's lodge and found everything in place, as though the occupant had merely stepped out for a moment to do some shopping in the market. The windows and doors were open, there were dirty cups in the sink, an unmade bed and an array of documents and open files on his large pine desk. Local police had completed their perfunctory search, posting a sentry outside the lodge, but since the suspect had been deported and there was no trial, the case had 'wrapped.'

Harvey had kept meticulous records and the scene of the crime revealed the full extent of the operation.

- Over six hundred photographs of naked boys.
- 331 cards in a comprehensive index filing system with the names of boys between seven and fourteen years old. The cards described sexual organs, acts boys would perform, and amounts of money spent on their clothing, books and haircuts.
- Over one hundred cards listed foreigners with details of their sexual preferences and the names of local boys they had been with.
- One card named a New York City man and read: 'Retired NYC truck mechanic now in jail in Mexico for "boys", 11. 82.'
- Another described an Australian who would 'try and come to PI (Philippine Islands) to live after completing a prison sentence.'
- Most of the names on the cards were regular tourists, though some cards listed businessmen in Manila connected to multinational companies; others were politicians, government officials and diplomats.

The activists were left exhausted and repulsed. It was like discovering the Marquis de Sade's diary.

Following Harvey's deportation, the impact was felt immediately in Pagsangan. A police raid, in February 1988, resulted in twenty-two suspects being rounded up: seven Americans, five West Germans, three Australians, two Belgians, a Briton, a Canadian, a Dutchman, a Japanese and a Spaniard.

Shay was given copies of the documents and he started the laborious task of preparing a counter index of the information, based on each individual's country. Once the details had been logged and cross-referenced, each file was copied and then mailed to the relevant police force. While on a visit to the US, Shay alerted the authorities to the files and they went after people on the list.

But Harvey, the man on the run, had disappeared and no one knew where he was hiding. Two years later, Shay was woken by a telephone call in the middle of the night. It was a journalist with news about the fugitive. The files Harvey left behind in Pagsangan had obligingly provided his own home address in the United States. With the information provided by Shay, local police acted on the tip and kept Harvey's house under surveillance.

Eventually, he showed up and the diligent police stake-out paid off. Harvey continued the abuse and was charged with twenty-three offences against children in the US. He was subsequently jailed. His past had caught up with him but his conviction was for abusing American children. He was never punished for his crimes against children in the Philippines.

He had got away.

2

Undercover 1995

I closed the door behind me and followed Stone inside. He walked in short jerky steps. Stone was in his late thirties, thickset, tousled hair, glasses, trainers, dressed casually.

The next forty minutes were one of the most excruciating episodes that I had ever experienced. Stone made it clear that my apparent interest in young girls wasn't unusual: anything that I desired was easily available, and he knew where to get it.

It was almost over. We walked back to the front door, he leaned sloppily forward as he turned the latch and opened it. It was dark outside and there was a fresh dampness in the air. The glow from a street lamp shone into the hallway where we were standing and cast long shadows down the passage.

It was almost over. Somehow I had to get over these final moments together, get past him, out of this place. But he was blocking the door.

I could feel a fresh breeze blow gently into the hallway where we stood. The equipment under my clothes felt heavy and cumbersome. Stone was staring intently at me. Could he see something? A wire sticking out of my collar at the back? A lead dangling out of trouser pocket? Bumps under my shirt?

For the first time during the encounter, I felt tense, apprehensive that he would uncover the secret recording device strapped to my body and the hidden camera in my tie. If he did, I sensed that he would attack me, but it also felt curiously exciting. Secretly, I hoped he'd hit me. I wanted him to grab the secret camera and shout at me. Because I wanted to strike him down. Within a few seconds, a great anger had welled up inside.

During my visit Stone had confirmed that he could arrange my 'sex tour'. He would lead me by the hand and take me to this land of perverted sex. He would take me himself. I could practice this repeatedly during my holiday with impunity. There would be no restrictions. There would be no worries from any authorities, should they see an adult man and a child. Stone would do this for me. He would do this for all his clients. This was his service. His personal service. He was proud of his credentials, his in-country network.

Could I take him on? I tried to recall the boxing moves of people such as Sonny Liston and Mike Tyson. Should I defend myself or go on the attack?

It happened fast. Stone reached out and touched my arm.

'Don't worry,' he said, reassuringly. 'We'll sort you out.'

He assumed that I was anxious about the trip and I had to convince him that he was right. I summoned up all my reserves to go after one last offensive to get him to repeat his boasts directly to my tie. 'But what if I can't find the girls or they're not that young?' I said, trying to keep my voice steady, detached from the anger that I was really feeling.

'I've told you, that's not a problem at all. Just tell me how young you want the girls.' He repeated his boasts in a matter of fact tone. 'I know people who can set this up.

It won't be a problem. But you've got to let me have the dates when you can go.'

Stone continually reminded me that he needed the dates for when I could travel. We shook hands and he stepped aside. He remarked on the cool breeze and thought the evenings were getting lighter. He hoped for good weather, a good summer.

I walked out of the house and into the night. All I could hear were my footsteps on the pavement, out of time with the rattle of recorders and cameras. I was no longer worried about wires and connections, about the pictures that my tie would capture or the sound quality being ruptured by the rustling of my clothes.

I just wanted to get away.

On the Trail

Fast Eddie gave me a hug. 'You did good.'

Adam was tense. He looked sternly at me. 'You were in there too long. We were worried. You shouldn't have stayed that long.'

'But there was nothing I could do,' I protested. 'He was on the phone to a client. I had to wait.'

'We were coming in to get you,' Adam replied.

We drove to a pub in Epsom and in the darkness of the car park they took me apart. The masking tape was gently ripped from my body and the equipment unplugged and replaced in the silver case. It stung. Fast Eddie was replaying the tape on the portable television. Stone's face stared back at me, askance at times, but he was on camera. There was relief all round. I knew I could convince him to talk to me but didn't know if I could master the technology. There had been a lot of instructions to remember. It was like getting into the driver's seat of a car for the first time while someone gives you a crash course in driving minutes before your test.

The next morning Adam phoned me at the office. He was pleased with the results but said that the picture focus on Stone had been erratic.

'What did you think of his friend?' Adam asked.

'What friend?' I replied.

'His friend who goes out to Thailand and the Philippines to pick up young girls.'

I was stunned. I couldn't recall anything like that.

'Well, it's on the tapes,' he confirmed. Adam gave me a summary of my conversation with Stone, just a few hours ago. I had no recollection of the exchange or of Stone referring to anyone else and neither could I recall my response.

'Who is this mystery man?'

All we had was a name. Peter.

The tapes had also revealed that Peter went out regularly four times a year. Christmas. Easter. Summer. Autumn. Adam speculated that he might be a teacher in a school or college.

'It fits with school terms,' he mused.

The conversation had centred around my apparent concern over trying to find very young girls on my own. I had expressed apprehension that the authorities would notice a man and a child. Stone reassured me with the network of contacts he already had and the ease with which he could get the job done. Why, he had done it many times before, and, my interests coincided with a good friend of his, Peter. Peter knew his way around. If I was concerned about things, then I could accompany them. They would look after me. But I would have to fit in with Peter's dates. He then told me when Peter usually travelled. Christmas. Easter. Summer. Autumn.

Our repulsion was tinged with rage but our wrath would accomplish very little. It had to be turned to strengthen our campaign. I knew what I had to do.

I called 747 Travel. With the tape recorder running.

It was a long call. Every few minutes, Stone would put me on hold while he dealt with inquiries; when it was a customer booking a trip, he'd ask me to call back. I did.

We had developed a rapport and chatted easily. My acting skills had been enhanced as I forced myself to be convincing as a potential 'difficult' customer seeking reassurance.

It worked. I had a name. I scribbled it down on a sheet of paper in front of me. Now I wanted to get out. Stone pressed me on dates. He mentioned a few.

'I'll get back to you,' I said.

I hung up the phone and dialled Adam at the television company. Over the next few days, we learned a lot about Stone's friend. He'd been traced to a block of flats in Sutton where he lived with his mother; his telephone number was ex-directory, he didn't have a police record, but he did have a van that he rented out. He was a lecturer and his college had been identified. It was in London.

It was clear that we had to go after him. But how could we make contact? Rent the van? Bump into him in the college? In the street? The TV company wanted me to invite Stone and Peter Mitchell to a meal in a particular restaurant where the table would be rigged with a hidden camera and recorder. But this was dropped. It was too risky. Unpredictable.

There was no option. I would have to go back to Stone.

Concerned that he would become annoyed at the time being wasted, I did as he requested. I came up with some dates. But this was conditional. I was spending a lot of money. I wanted reassurance that this was going to be worth it. I wanted reassurance from someone who had done this before. I wanted reassurance from his friend. Peter Mitchell. In person.

It took some haggling but eventually Stone agreed to talk to Mitchell.

'I can't be sure he'll do it but I'll ask him if he'll meet you,' Stone said, struggling to contain his irritation. 'Call me on Monday. We're meeting for a drink at the weekend.'

It worked. Mitchell had said he'd call me. Probably. He would call on Thursday evening. Late.

The television company allowed me to use a room around the corner from their studios on Euston Road but they raised the stakes. It wasn't enough to get him on the phone. We had to get him on camera. We had to meet.

The room was part of an office unit that ITV used and it was crammed full of files and merchandising from old television programmes. There were two desks back to back and several phones but only one was plugged in to a tape recorder. The first hour passed. It was important not to get distracted and to stay prayerfully focused. 'Lord, I can't do this without you,' I said aloud. I never felt a grip on my body or a touch on my hand resting on the telephone. But neither was I seized by panic. I was holding the pattern. Just about.

The second hour passed. It was getting late. He had forgotten. He had the wrong date. He had the wrong time. He had scribbled down the wrong number. He had left it in a shirt that was in the washing machine. Stone had lied to me. He'd never given Mitchell the message. Mitchell had lied to Stone. Yeah. Yeah. Yeah. He had no intention of making the call. Mitchell was enraged with Stone. You told him what? Why did you tell him I did that? Who is he?

The phone rang.

It was Peter Mitchell. He was different to Stone. He was sharp, cautious, brusque, and not eager to talk. All he would admit to was using 747 Travel to get cheap flights. That's all he knew. And, grudgingly, he agreed to help me if we met in some exotic location. Help me, if he could.

There was nothing on the tape that could incriminate him to anything that we'd discussed. He was too smart. The call had been a failure. Lord…

And just before the final click of the telephone, a glimmer. Unexpectedly, he agreed to meet. Well, maybe.

Mitchell told me that he'd be in a pub in Epsom on Sunday night. If I wanted to buy him a pint, he wouldn't object.

'I'll be there around eight. I'll be there for about fifteen minutes.'

He hung up.

Manhunt in the Philippines

It was a big operation and we met at three o'clock at the Pizza Hut on South Street in Epsom. Fast Eddie was on a job and Adam Holloway, an investigative television reporter with several major documentaries under his belt, took his place. Adam was in charge and we reviewed the information. He thought the story was developing well and would make an important segment within *News at Ten*. The government would have to take notice. They would have to do something. But the next few hours were decisive as Mitchell would have to talk on camera. And this time they wanted clear footage of him outside the pub. Adam told me that I would have to leave the pub with him and keep him talking outside while facing the van with masked out windows.

I couldn't eat anything.

I was ready for the set up, and once again, I stripped in one of Epsom's many cul-de-sacs. It was dark and no one looked twice. They checked me for sound and pictures. We were on.

Just before I reached my car, Adam Holloway dashed over, ruffled my shirt, brushed me down quite forcefully, and then gave me a playful tap on my cheek. 'You'll be fine,' he said, reassuringly.

Mitchell was dead on time and easy to spot. A large hulking figure, he looked sweaty and unfriendly. He asked for Fosters and when I returned with two pints, he directed me to the rear of the pub which was deserted. I'd told him that I'd be holding a copy of the *Sunday Times* and I placed the paper on the table in front of us.

Mitchell looked at the paper and said gruffly, 'You're not from the press, are you?'

It was a shaky start but things got better. He declined my offer of a second pint of Fosters but during our half hour together he accepted my cover story. He told me that he was a frequent visitor and regularly used 747 Travel's cheap fares, once for a long weekend, because the tickets were so cheap.

Mitchell knew what I wanted and ran through the scene, and then showed me pictures of a hotel that he part-owned. But he wasn't a property tycoon, he was a sex tourist. He was involved, and though he talked guardedly, he incriminated himself during our meeting.

As we stepped out of the pub, I asked him what car he drove, and we lingered on the steps discussing vehicles while facing the nondescript van with blacked out windows.

The ordeal was over. Mitchell got in his black Ford and drove off in the direction of Stone's house. He never noticed a black motorbike take off at the same time but set well back.

The next day Adam told me that the camera hadn't picked up any pictures but they could still use the piece because the sound quality was good. They had footage of Mitchell outside the pub and intended to film Stone and Mitchell together when we confirmed the booking. The idea was to follow it through by accompanying them to Thailand before confronting them. The trip was scheduled for late December. It was difficult to contemplate being away from the family at Christmas, especially on such an assignment, but it was equally hard to know that Stone, Mitchell and their crowd would be in a faraway land, abusing girls and women, possibly even on Christmas Day.

Then the TV people pulled out of the Christmas trip and told us they would pick up the story in the new year. One Saturday in February, Adam Chadwick rang me at home and said, 'We need to talk. There have been some developments.'

Adam was blunt. ITV news had hooked up with another group who had recently started a similar investigation. We would still be included as part of the story but the Stone/Mitchell investigation was on hold.

It was a blow. ITV had approached us and we had turned down other media so that we could work exclusively with them. But the biggest concern was that Stone and Mitchell were fading into the distance. However, Adam didn't have time for a discussion.

Adam Holloway led the investigation that centred on Paradise Express, a travel agency owned by Michael Clarke, in Eastbourne. He had advertised in *Exchange & Mart*, soliciting for customers to an 'Adult Disneyland' in the Philippines. Things moved quickly. Clarke was videotaped in Eastbourne, on a hidden camera, promising young girls and was thrilled that Holloway and his 'friend' signed up. The other group linked up with Shay and dates were confirmed.

It was tough watching 'our story' get taken over and worrying that ITV seemed to be stonewalling whenever the subject of Stone and Mitchell came up. On the morning that we were due to leave for the Philippines I pulled out, concluding that this wasn't the best use of my time. My role had become one of an observer and Adam Holloway couldn't confirm that they would use me. When I phoned Shay to explain, he said, 'That's an answer to prayer.' For separate reasons, he had become wary of the situation, though he was committed to the investigation of Clarke.

Clarke led the pair through the sex industry in the Philippines and their covert undercover filming was successful. The final scene was a confrontation on the beach when Adam Holloway revealed he was not a sex tourist but an undercover reporter. With the television cameras still rolling, Michael Clarke erupted, denied the charges, and stormed off.

ITV were wrapping up the story and called for confirmation on specific details as they were completing the final edit. I asked Adam if he could include something about Stone and Mitchell. He said he'd try but didn't hold out much hope.

The story was broadcast on ITV news, with prominent coverage about Jubilee Campaign and an interview with me. This significant coverage was probably the first time that a top news programme had linked the key components of the issue. The news report demonstrated how easy it was for British sex tourists to abuse children without restrictions, getting away with it the way Paradise Express had done.

The programme caused a little tremor around the country. We got telephone calls and letters from people everywhere expressing support for our campaign to see the law changed in Britain. We urged them to write to the Prime Minister, John Major, and to their local Member of Parliament, and many did, sending us copies of their letters.

The Advertising Director of *Exchange & Mart* said he was sickened that his reputable publication had been exploited in this way. He'd be fired if this was repeated and he asked for our help in monitoring the magazine's advertising content.

'You've got something else in there that we're concerned about,' I said, and gave him the page number of Stone's advert in *Exchange & Mart*. Although not as sexually explicit as 'Adult Disneyland', it gave a hint at what was on offer.

The Advertising Director said he'd take a look into it, but asked, 'Do you have any evidence?'

'*We* don't.' My frustration was carried in the exaggerated emphasis on the word 'we'. There was evidence. 'We' didn't have it. ITV did.

I called the office of *News at Ten* but nothing had changed so this time I asked if they would turn over the tapes to us. ITV discussed it with 'upstairs' but the request was refused. No explanation was given.

In the Philippines, the Paradise Express operation had closed down, Clarke had disappeared. CNN in the Philippines had broadcast an edited version of ITV's news special and it rocked the country. A nationwide manhunt was announced: FIND MICHAEL CLARKE! But the police had no leads and the bars were covering their tracks. No one knew anything.

He had got away.

* * * *

Although we hadn't pumped out much publicity following the feature on *News at Ten*, several journalists called wanting to join us on a similar story. But these investigations were time-consuming, and we still had hopes of reviving the 747 Travel story with ITV.

A friend in the media introduced me to Roger Insall, a reporter at the *News of the World*, and after an initial meeting at their Wapping office, he suggested that we link up. Although I was apprehensive, knowing the reputation of the *News of the World*, and the rumours of how the tabloid press snared their suspects, I felt the risk was worth taking. Roger was a veteran journalist with a genuine interest in this issue. Also, he worked for the newspaper with the largest circulation in Britain. If we wanted to get the attention of the politicians in Westminster, this would be a fantastic platform.

Roger called a few days later and as we reviewed things, three clear stories emerged. Firstly, there was the Australian, Victor Fitzgerald, whose arrest Shay had videotaped. Secondly, Roger had located Clarke's business partner in Paradise Express. Thirdly, another target, whom he didn't identify, was linked to a television soap star. 'It's a long shot but I'm on the trail,' he said.

The hint of a scandal linked to a celebrity was enough of a hook for the newspaper to turn up the heat. The *News of the World* wanted the story. And they wanted it now. Roger said, 'I'm leaving in two days. Are you in?'

3

Investigation

It's a double whammy. Manila's dry heat socked me as we landed, leaving me parched, while the humidity crept in like a sneaking fog and drained any energy that was left. But the courtesy car from the airport was 'air-con', a popular, ubiquitous, phrase, and the air-conditioned drive to the hotel was pleasant.

The city's gigantic garbage dump, that had spawned a virtual shanty town scavenging from it, had been cleared from its site. The cab's driver explained the reason. 'It offended the tourists.'

'What happened to the people?' The squatter camp had been documented by photographers and reporters showing the squalid life of families forced to survive on the remains of the city.

'Gone,' he chuckled, gesticulating with his hand, a flicking movement to convey something that had been hurtled into the oblivion of Manila's unknown.

We talked a little, or rather, he talked, and I nodded with regularity. Ascertaining that I was a lone male, on an anonymous visit mixing business and a holiday, he said, 'If you want a nice friendly girl, I can fix it. I'm always at the hotel. Just tell reception that you want a car and ask for Frankie as your driver.'

Frankie had simplified things and it was easy to see how travellers could drift into unexpected scenarios. With poverty at epidemic levels, the pressure to deliver was heightened, confirming that the trade would be driven by the demand. Frankie had done this before and he made it clear that he could fix anything I wanted. It was a chilling welcome to Manila.

Roger Insall had flown in earlier with the *News of the World* photographer, Alistair Pullen, but they weren't in their room so I left a message for them at reception.

When I dialled Shay's number in Olongapo City, he was in the midst of an operation, talking fast, interrupting our conversation every few minutes to bark out messages to someone with him.

'Guess what?' Shay yelled over the phone. 'Michael Clarke is hiding out here. The Paradise Express operation has blown up.'

'Did the police trace him?'

'No,' Shay remarked. 'I've just had a tip-off. But we've got to be careful or he'll slip out of the net, pay off a corrupt policeman, and get away.'

Shay explained that they knew where Clarke was hiding and that he was waiting for a trusted policeman so that they could make the arrest together.

'He's going to be arrested tonight or tomorrow at dawn,' Shay said. 'How quickly can you get down to Olongapo?'

Not quickly enough.

While I was on the phone to Shay, Roger had called my room. They were at the bar. The news about Clarke was important. Roger needed a few stories with British links to ensure that the paper definitely ran his piece, but when we checked logistics, geography and travel arrangements, it was clear that we couldn't make the journey in time.

When I phoned Shay back, he'd already left on the stake-out, with agents from the National Bureau of Investigation (NBI).

Later that night, Shay confirmed that Clarke had been arrested. 'They got him,' Shay said firmly. 'He didn't get away. I think they're taking him back to Manila tonight or maybe early tomorrow morning.'

On hearing the news, the three of us headed out to the NBI headquarters but no one knew anything about the arrest. Around midnight, Roger decided we should scout out the clubs downtown, in Makati and Ermita. He'd been here before, on other stories, and knew his way around. There were foreigners in most of the bars, drinking with the girls, fooling around. It wasn't particularly busy, and the girls had time to talk. The girls asked us to buy them drinks so Roger pulled out a fistful of Filipino dollars, and everyone was a friend. Roger learned that the city had been cleaned up in a recent crusade to outlaw prostitution, but in reality little had changed. It had been driven underground, into private houses or out of town.

In a back street dingy club, an older woman came over and asked if any of the girls around the room interested me. Following Roger's line, I asked if there were any younger girls available. The woman wagged her finger in the air, in a mock scolding motion, and said there were many sixteen year old girls nearby, but she could have someone younger the next day. 'I can bring you a girl who is about eleven or twelve years old, but you'll have to see her in the evening because she's still at school.' The woman scribbled her name and phone number on a card and handed it to me.

The ease with which the line shifted between women, teenagers and younger girls wasn't hard to comprehend as events unfolded in front of us. Everyone wanted to please and it would take strength and resolve for some to remain resolute. Every step led down and along the way there was always someone to take their hand.

I'd fought and lost a battle with jet lag and was relieved when Roger decided that he'd caught enough of Manila's low life for 'background'.

It was a late night.

Shay arrived at our hotel the following morning and we headed off for the NBI offices where Clarke was expected. We were forced to wait for some time at reception and positioned ourselves under the ceiling fan. Michael Clarke was inside. The dye in his hair had started to fade but he had showered, shaved, and, dressed in a grey stripe suit, looked slim, slinky and smart. He sat under a fan, like everyone else, trying to stay cool, but he was nervous and fidgety. When the sentry outside the room was called away, we slipped in, and Roger got to work on Clarke. He knew that time was short and that Clarke could be summoned away at a moment's notice. Clarke was hesitant at first, but a few words from Roger put him at ease. He started to talk.

Clarke told Roger his side of the story, though I suspected that he didn't know that his new best friend was a journalist from Britain's top-selling newspaper. My chair was positioned nearby and I could hear most of their conversation, while Alistair moved around the room sneaking shots of Clarke and Roger without either noticing. The room was busy with detectives checking records and clerks with forms to be filled in, but Roger had taken command and it was an impressive performance. He insisted that he should finish questioning the suspect first and curiously they accepted his word.

Suddenly, the door swung open, and a television crew with a hoard of reporters burst into the room. The media invasion was launched with a barrage of questions.

Clarke looked terrified, covering his face with a newspaper, while Roger went mad. In a moment of twisted irony, he pushed me forward to face the mob from the media. 'Deal with them,' he said.

Turning to face a scrum of charging television cameras and reporters and perplexed at my promotion by Roger, I was surprised by my powers of persuasion: they appeared to halt and stared at me for an instant. Holding up my hands, I advanced and mysteriously they retreated, while some aggressive journalists offered some half-hearted resistance.

'Who are you?' the television reporter yelled, while his lights man shoved the spotlight on me.

'Are you his lawyer?' someone shouted out.

'No comment,' I replied confidently. 'You can't stay here. You must leave now.'

Astonishingly, they complied.

Michael Clarke in police custody, giving interviews to the press.   Photo: Danny Smith

Inside the room, the pressure intensified. Alistair got to work in earnest, positioning himself beside Roger, moving closer to the target without distracting him. Clarke produced a list of customers, pages and pages of people in Britain who had written to Paradise Express for a catalogue of 'Adult Disneyland' pleasures. Roger summoned one of the detectives and insisted that the document be copied immediately, while the police officer, in turn, grabbed one of the clerks and the man rushed off on his assignment.

Bedlam erupted again as the reporters and television crew forced their way back in. They yelled out questions to Clarke at the other end of the room. He yelled back. The chaos was observed with bemused detachment by NBI detectives who wandered in and out, bewildered by Roger who had totally taken charge in a *tour de force* performance.

Clarke was now holding his own press conference, telling anyone who would listen that he was a victim of a religious cult, Jubilee Campaign, about an Irish priest, who was a trouble maker, and a certain Danny Smith who had set him up. Clarke swore on his daughter's life that he was innocent. It was evident that Clarke had heard about ITV's *News* report but hadn't seen it or he would have recognised me.

The television crew cornered Shay in one part of the room and recorded an interview, while Roger told Clarke that he was a journalist. Clarke took it on the chin, unfazed, and distilled a 'message for British readers', unrolling his 'innocence and set up by unscrupulous cult members' communiqué.

At one point, while in conversation with Roger, Clarke turned to me, and extended his hand, 'I didn't get your name.'

'Dan,' I replied, enigmatically.

Roger had obtained an interview with Clarke and decided that it was time to move on. We left Shay with the media buzzing around him, and headed for Angeles City, about two hours away.

On the journey, Roger kept us enthralled with details of scoops and exposés.

Tabloid journalists have a bad reputation, but his perspective was that fame, greed, money (or, rather, the love of it), deceit, sleaze and revenge were among the motives that drove people to the media with secrets about former friends, acquaintances and chance encounters. Over the last decade, he had played the role of a crusading journalist exposing the crooked and wayward among churchmen, politicians and entertainers. His reports had resulted in arrests and deportations and, in one instance in Colombia, almost ended in his assassination. He literally raced to the airport and caught the first plane leaving the terminal.

Roger went undercover and played a major role in exposing the notorious Paedophile Information Service, a network of some of the worst offenders dedicated to abusing very young children. Roger was tipped off that one of their leaders was hiding out in Belgium and he camped outside his house. The offender, annoyed at the harassment, complained to the local police about the irritation. Roger was arrested but quickly released when he explained the focus of his interest. The offender was unknown in Belgium, but aware that his newspaper's deadline was looming, Roger came up with a brilliant ruse on the spot. The police went along with it, called the offender and told him that they had caught the man who had been annoying him but he was needed to identify the culprit before they could formally press charges. Would he mind coming down to the police station, a police vehicle would be provided to transport him.

Very kindly, sir. It worked, and the man walked into the station to find a pair of handcuffs with his initials on, waiting for him.

Alistair had his own stories as a photographer with the tabloids. He was the man who had shot the first photograph that was printed in the press of Prince Charles with his mistress, Camilla Parker Bowles. Significantly, this was the first time that the couple had been photographed together since the death of Princess Diana and was considered an important landmark in the curious royal relationship.

'How hard was it to get that photograph?' I asked. 'Did you have to wait for hours?'

'Not at all,' he laughed. 'It was one of the easiest pictures to get. They – or someone close to them – had tipped us off to be at a particular spot at a certain time. All that I had to do was turn up with my camera with a long lens.'

The ride was entertaining and passed quickly. We checked in at the Oasis, one of the better hotels in Angeles but still a dump. It was a common sight to see local girls returning with foreign guests. Downtown, the clubs were sleazy, the girls young, with foreigners everywhere. Roger was out on the prowl, hoping that the trail would lead to The Target he'd pursued. The Target was linked to a television soap star. Getting the story into the paper depended on his success with The Target.

He returned at midday. The Target had agreed to meet him that night. Roger and Alistair were part of the cover story that had been concocted. I was out of it. 'Sorry, mate,' Roger said. 'Next time.' The encounter was going to happen at the Cock'n'Bull, a sleazy go-go bar on the strip owned by a British man. Roger told me that he would return to the hotel at 9.30pm to pick me up and we'd go out together to follow up some other leads.

If I wanted to hang out at the Cock'n'Bull, he would try to engineer a collision. I considered the options but felt prompted not to leave the hotel.

Roger returned three hours late, at midnight.

'You're just not going to believe what happened,' he said, charging into the room. Walking around in an agitated state, he related a convoluted but astonishing story.

Roger met The Target through the bar owner of the Cock'n'Bull, whose confidence he had won by claiming to know Paradise Express's business partner (Bruce Teasdale, in London). Every story that Roger told was linked to Paradise Express and Bruce. The trick worked because the club owner also knew Bruce. As a result of this apparent connection, Roger was welcomed into the circle and The Target started to talk. A local photographer clicked away, light bulbs flashing. It worked like a dream. The set-up had taken several hours but it was in the bag.

Almost.

Roger set the scene. He and The Target were with the owner of the Cock'n'Bull in his club. Roger was buying. They raised their glasses, again. It was party time.

A stranger walked into the bar and over to Roger, The Target, and the club owner. The club owner exclaimed, 'Bruce! What are you doing here?'

'I've just flown in. Who's this?' Bruce said, jet lagged and exhausted, pointing at Roger.

The Target slammed his glass on the bar, going crazy. 'Whaddya mean? This is Roger, your friend from Thailand.'

'Friend? I've never seen him before in my life!'

It was Paradise Express's business partner, Bruce Teasdale, who had just arrived from London. Roger's alleged connection with Bruce looked like being shown up as the ruse it was.

The next few minutes were tense, the risk obvious. The owner of the Cock'n'Bull called on the local muscle. Roger and Alistair were surrounded.

With seconds to spare, Roger declared conspiratorially, 'I'm going to tell you everything. I'm really after Michael Clarke,' he said. 'He owes me money and I'm going to get him.'

Alistair was introduced as Roger's 'hit man' who would earn his wages if Clarke didn't pay up.

Complicated manoeuvres followed but somehow Roger got out of the club.

Roger explained that Alistair had been unable to get photographs of The Target, but they used a local photographer, Ricky Lee, who hung around the clubs and bars, to get the incriminating pictures. They had to get prints. Without prints, the *News of the World* would not run the story. The hunt was on now to find Ricky Lee and to get the photographs that he had taken earlier that night. If the Target, Bruce or anyone else realised what was happening, no one would leave town.

Roger, Alistair and I jumped in a cab and headed for the strip. The conversation was fast and furious, the general assumption being that the Paradise Express business partner had flown in from London to clean up the Philippine end of the operation.

Roger told me that Bruce had brought a copy of ITV's news report on video with him. Like a light bulb exploding before us, we realised that if Bruce had a copy of the news video, then he knew what I looked like. But I would be unable to recognise him. Roger pointed a finger at me and grinned. I was in the TV news report and if I had gone down to the club, and had been with Roger when Bruce burst in, his cover story would have lasted seconds, with no telling as to what might have happened.

We had to move fast. Find Ricky Lee, the photographer. Get the film. Get out.

We hit the clubs. Things were still buzzing. But Ricky Lee wasn't in any of the bars.

The only place we hadn't checked out was the Cock'n'Bull, the bar where Bruce Teasdale was drinking. Alistair agreed to step back into the danger zone. He packed a swagger, acted out the role of Roger's 'hit man', and was back in minutes with the news that Roger's cover story was holding. Just. But, still no photographer.

Finally, we met a bouncer from one of the clubs who recognised Roger and told him that Ricky Lee had gone home around midnight. The bouncer knew where the photographer lived and offered to pick up the roll of film and a deal was struck. Half the money now. The other half when the bouncer produced the film. They arranged to meet at the Oasis at noon.

It had been a late, late night, and no one spoke on the taxi ride back to the hotel.

*   *   *   *

I've never liked early mornings and when Alistair phoned my room at 8 am, I grumbled. Roger had showered and was in the lobby. Like a good newspaperman, he had all the dailies with him and Clarke's arrest was blasted across the front pages of most of them. The *Philippine Star's* report stated

> Travel agent Michael Clarke, 49, wept when confronted by NBI agents at Luz's Place in Baloy Beach.
>
> 'I deny all allegations made against me,' Clarke of Eastbourne in Sussex, said in a statement. 'I swear to God and on my only daughter's life that I am telling the truth.'

An NBI agent said they still had no evidence against Clarke and could not charge him criminally. Sen Ernesto Herrera, however, urged the NBI to use video footage of Clarke taken by the Independent Television [News] which could implicate the Briton.

Clarke claimed the video footage had been 'doctored' by a certain Danny Smith who belongs to a religious group called Jubilee Campaign.

Herrera had alerted the NBI about Clarke and contacted Columban priest Fr Shay Cullen, who operates a child protection programme at the Preda Foundation. Preda members led the NBI agents to Baloy Beach.

All the papers carried a similar report. Clarke denied the charges. He had been set up. He had been set up by Danny Smith. He had been set up by a religious cult, Jubilee Campaign. He had been set up and the police had no evidence to charge him. He had been set up.

Clarke's case was the talk of the hotel in Angeles. I overheard two guys talking at the bar discussing what they would do to the villain who had framed him. I didn't linger.

Roger was focused on his story and was going to wait in Angeles for the photographer from the Cock'n'Bull; and he needed to see The Target, one final time. It was high risk but he needed one final quote.

Alistair and I hit the road to Olongapo City where Shay was expecting us. The rolling hills and greenery were pleasant and Alistair was talkative in the car. Cynical and critical. What did I want? Fame? Fortune? He was suspicious of people like me and named the frauds and hypocrites he had encountered while working in the media.

I never pulled any punches, didn't repeat clichéd jargon or tired old phrases but told him that my family and my personal faith were the important things in my life.

I understood his frustration with Christian groups who treated people like him as a target. I sometimes felt uncomfortable that the Christian faith was marketed as though we belonged to an exclusive club where people smiled brighter than anyone else or had better hairstyles and through this became better people. Though well-intentioned, such exclusiveness could be interpreted as triumphalism, a kind of spiritual snobbery.

I didn't want to become part of the hype and advertising related to the business of Christianity and found it difficult to fit into the mainstream of church activity. Bob Dylan summarised this aptly when he wrote: 'If Jesus returned today, Christianity would start all over again.'

My mother had taken me to church as a child but an unexpected meeting with George Verwer led me to personal faith. I spent time on Operation Mobilisation and those early years gave me a strong foundation that helped me withstand the stormy turbulence of life and to overcome residual cynicism from encounters within the politics of church life. I have come to understand that my spiritual experience has been about the journey of faith and not about a state of arrival. My spirituality is about a relationship with God, strong and real, personal and precious. That's what is important to me.

Alistair told me that the important things in his life were his material possessions. 'It's about how much money I can make,' he said. 'Getting there before anyone else. Beating them to the punch.'

We explored the motivation of people and considered that even the hardened outlaw was seeking redemption, even though they didn't know it. We talked about Martin Scorsese's downbeat movie, *Taxi Driver*, and the loner, outsider, stalker, Travis Bickle (Robert de Niro), who became obsessed with a child prostitute, played by Jodie Foster, and decided that his life's work was to rescue her from the clutches of her pimp. The film ended in a bloodbath. I cranked out a line from Dylan's epic song, *Lily, Rosemary and the Jack of Hearts*, in which one of the characters, Rosemary, is described as someone who was 'looking to do one good deed before she died'.

'Perhaps a day will come,' I told him, 'that you will care about something, that you will want to help someone. And when that day comes, you'll remember this conversation.'

'No. No. No,' he laughed. 'Not me. That day isn't in my calendar.'

We decided on a pint of Guinness to settle the bet.

Olongapo had the eerie atmosphere of a lost, forgotten city that had been left to decay slowly. Old American style automobiles lay rusting by the side of the road, shiny Jeepneys picked up passengers, standing by rickety buildings with the paint peeling, while familiar global advertising brands, such as CocaCola, assured travellers of the road that everything's gonna be all right.

Although Shay and I had developed a close relationship, this was my first visit to the Preda Foundation. Lex and Merle Hermosa, who set up the Centre with Shay, were an outstanding couple and together they had developed a dedicated team and an efficient system. Even Alistair was impressed and drawn into the work.

Shay's one room office/bedroom had a veranda with a spectacular view of the bay where we were served the best fried fish I'd ever tasted, with delicious mangoes for dessert.

The phone rang. It was Roger in Angeles. The photographer didn't show. Alistair had to return to Angeles to re-shoot the photos and recreate the missing scenes with the suspects. Alistair shuffled. 'How can we do it?' he asked on the telephone. 'Any way we can,' answered Roger. It was the same deal. The paper couldn't run the story without photos.

Within the hour, Alistair had gone, and Shay and I caught up with news. We were on the balcony when the phone rang, but he was back, minutes later, frowning. Another threat but he shrugged it off. Ten minutes later, the phone rang again. The latest news was that Michael Clarke might be released. This galvanised him into action, writing letters to politicians, police authorities, newspapers, and the swirl of the fax machine pumped the protest into the night.

But it was getting too late for me. I left him at the fax machine.

* * * *

The next day was an important one and everyone at Preda busied themselves preparing for one more day in court against two offenders: the Australian, Victor Fitzgerald and a Frenchman called Charlie Luton.

Fiztgerald's story was compelling. An Australian tourist, he sailed into Subic Bay and dropped anchor just below the Preda Centre. Shay was on the balcony when he spotted young kids on board a yacht with a *farrang* (foreigner).

The law prohibited young children being in a private place with a foreigner who wasn't a blood relation. That was the law: it wasn't always enforced. Shay's suspicion was confirmed when he grabbed a pair of binoculars and could see the Australian on the yacht with the young children.

He kept watch and within a short time was certain that things weren't right. He phoned the police. When they arrived, the officer in charge was reluctant to act. But Shay wasn't surprised. Sometimes officials preferred such encounters to be handled quietly, giving the offender the opportunity to buy his way out of a tight spot. With the Australian's yacht docked so close, Shay was adamant. 'Arrest him now or I will do it myself – a citizen's arrest.'

With no option, the officer took over a local fishing boat and boarded the yacht where Victor Fitzgerald was caught on board with three children, one just seven years old. The difference with this encounter was that the entire incident was captured on video, including the exchange between Shay and the diffident police officer.

I knew the case well because I had seen the videotape and had tried to interest the British media in it, but was told the story didn't have legs. Fitzgerald wasn't British. As a result, as already mentioned, we had started our own investigation.

Accusation and counter accusation complicated matters but eventually Fitzgerald was charged with

The police, forced by Shay, approach Fitzgerald's yacht.
Photo: Father Shay Cullen

attempted rape against a young teen called Gloria. Her family were pressured to get Gloria to drop charges and, to ensure that she could not attend a crucial hearing, they manacled her feet with a dog chain and locked her in an outhouse. With the leading witness missing, the case would have been dropped and the Australian would have disappeared. After three days of captivity, Gloria escaped by climbing through a window and hobbling to the Preda Centre, with the chains still around her feet.

Shay worked with the local Chief Prosecutor and despite intense pressure, Fitzgerald eventually faced the court. This hearing was critical as Shay's videotape of Fitzgerald's arrest was due to be screened for the judge.

The courtroom was a short journey and Preda's investigators were there. It took two workers to carry the

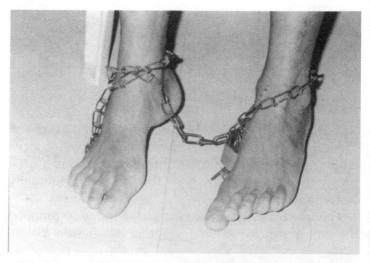

Gloria was held captive with a dog chain to prevent her from giving evidence.

Photo: Father Shay Cullen

bulky television into the courtroom while Shay guarded the videotape. The courtroom was a fairly small room with a porch, six rows of benches and a raised platform for the judicial authorities.

It was hot inside the courtroom, so we stood under the low roof, seeking shelter from the intense heat. Fitzgerald and the Frenchman, Charlie Luton, arrived in a police vehicle, both wandering around unchecked. Luton was surly but Fitzgerald looked harmless. He was friendly with the guards, strolled over to the tea shop across the road, bought a Coke, meandered back and forth.

Fitzgerald sauntered over to me and started a conversation, while I played the part of a curious onlooker. Nothing he said was surprising and, predictably, he blamed everything on Shay, whom he cursed frequently, while referring to him as a 'correspondent from *Time* magazine.' We talked for about forty minutes and he let slip that he had a daughter studying in London. He mumbled, 'But they don't want to know me. That bastard has ruined my life.' He cut a forlorn and dishevelled figure, and a twinge of sympathy hit me while a shadow of doubt crept in. I wondered if this apparently kindly old man could have been misunderstood.

Word came down the line that Fitzgerald's hearing had been postponed, much to the frustration of the Preda workers. They were convinced that it was a tactic employed by the defence attorneys to de-fragment the prosecution's case, in the hope that it would eventually be forgotten.

There was a flurry of activity as the judge summoned the courtroom to order. Fitzgerald sat beside Luton, whose case started after several requests for postponement from the Frenchman's attorney.

Luton had a cold, icy stare. He was wiry, tough, a karate expert, with a military background and rumour had it that he had served with the French Foreign Legion. He had apparently admitted to killings back home, and had been jailed in France for sex offences against his son. Everyone called him 'Crazy Charlie'.

Crazy Charlie was annoyed with me because I took his photograph while he sat outside in the tea shop with Fitzgerald, and he had complained to a police officer. In court, he continually made eye contact, stared, walked across the room and taunted me with a piece of paper. He walked with a swagger and appeared the most confident person in the courtroom. Crazy Charlie had been charged with sexual offences against a young boy, Allen, whom he had legally adopted in Olongapo. Allen, a tiny figure, aged about ten or eleven, walked forward to give evidence and hunched over in the witness chair. Towering over him, Luton's attorney was determined to intimidate him, speaking in a loud voice, and repeatedly pointing his finger at the child in a threatening manner. But the city prosecutor was impressive and the judge sympathetic; although Luton's attorney was admonished for his grandstanding, he seemed to take little notice.

The ordeal was over and Allen stepped down from the witness stand but was forced to pass both Luton and Fitzgerald, seated in the front row. As he walked past, the child threw a piece of paper at Luton, in rage and frustration, and then crumpled in tears on a bench behind us. It was a poignant but electric moment.

Luton's lawyer eventually succeeded in gaining a postponement and another court hearing was set for three weeks' time. Meanwhile Fitzgerald's case hadn't even been heard even though their leading witness, Gloria, was seated alongside us.

The day in court was over. In frustration, Preda staff loaded the television and video back into the vehicle, while the noonday sun beat down on us, sparing no one.

Crazy Charlie came down the steps of the courtroom and headed directly for me. His eyes, cold and steady, betrayed his anger. It seemed that a violent confrontation was inevitable and I prepared for some kind of assault. Crazy Charlie walked right up to me till we were almost touching and yelled into my face, his eyes fierce with anger, never leaving mine. He demanded to know who I was and why I was taking his photograph. Unprepared for the confrontation, I held my ground, determined not to be intimidated. He continued to stare, eyeball to eyeball, but my response seemed to keep him in check. No one intervened but he ended the confrontation by threatening to file a complaint against me. I challenged him to do so and he stormed off to find his lawyer.

Meanwhile, Gloria came out of the courtroom. She was a slim, elegant girl, about fourteen years old. Fitzgerald was facing a charge of attempted rape against her, and he watched her intensively as she walked across our path and climbed into a maroon Space-Wagon type vehicle. As the vehicle pulled out, I observed Fitzgerald closely. The body language and facial expression were unmistakable. He was enraptured, almost mesmerised, and followed her movements, barely blinking, completely obsessed, watching the Space Wagon till it was out of sight. It was this eerie spectacle, captured in a private moment, that convinced me that his look of affection was not one of a parent but of a lover.

The next day, a police vehicle with senior NBI officials from Manila pulled up unexpectedly at Preda's office. They requested a meeting about Paradise Express and Michael Clarke and we sat down on smart cane chairs in a room on the ground floor, with the fine linen curtains gently blowing in the breeze.

Shay's frustration was evident when it emerged that the case against Clarke was slipping away because of alleged police bungling. The tables were turned. The priest was quizzing the police. Had the police searched the house where Clarke was hiding? No. Did they know what had happened to the evidence that was in the house? It had probably vanished. Had they seen the promotional brochure from Paradise Express advertising an 'Adult Disneyland'? No. How much did they know about Clarke? Very little. Had ITV's reporters given them the tapes of their interviews with Clarke? No. Did they know that Paradise Express's business partner, Bruce Teasdale, had arrived in the Philippines and was currently in Angeles City? No.

I handed over copies of Paradise Express's advertisement from *Exchange & Mart* and the NBI officers examined this for the first time. Clarke had denied all the charges against him, insisting that he had been set up, but the officers agreed that the documents were incriminating. We described the contents of ITV's news programme and for the first time they learned that Clarke had been recorded on videotape offering young girls in the Philippines for sex.

Shay thought that something could be salvaged if they moved quickly and the NBI officers agreed to act on his advice. The NBI chief authorised me to collect the unedited video from ITV *News at Ten* and a letter would be prepared for me to carry back to London.

* * * *

On my last night in Olongapo, Shay took me on a tour of the city's night life. Bars, massage parlours and dance clubs were scattered around but the action was moving to Baloy Beach, now referred to as the new Pattaya, Thailand's notorious sex district.

Shay pointed out the building where Clarke was arrested and then pulled up at a bar called Mr

Pumpernickels. It was a scene straight out of an Elmore Leonard novel. The joint's owner, Harry Jost, welcomed us like old friends. Girls with heavily painted faces walked past. At the bar, a man with greasy long hair and tattoos on his arms eyed us without looking up. Two teenage girls, one in hot pants, the other a pink micro skirt, walked in, waved to Harry and stood by the bar. Two ice cold Sao Miguels appeared mysteriously before them. The girls looked at us and giggled. Postcards from around the world were clipped to the side of the bar. Messages with cards and notes were pinned to a wooden post. A sign at the corner said, 'Rooms to Rent'. The jukebox blasted out a repetitive loop of songs, mostly disco.

Harry talked about arrests, kickbacks to corrupt politicians, wanted men's secrets. He was called away to the bar and Shay whispered to me that he was the source who tipped him off about Clarke's hideaway. When he returned, Harry said he knew where the girls featured in the TV *News* programme had been taken.

'I'm going to rescue the girls and bring them to Preda,' he declared.

He had a lot of information about Clarke and spoke confidently. Clarke had offered him a slice of the action. Clarke told him that they would make a lot of money from setting up Paradise Express. Everyone wanted to come on his tours. All Harry would have to do was to allow the sex tourists to stay at his place, hang out, have a beer, and of course, have some young girls available.

'Michael Clarke said he'd make a fortune but the first customers he brought were reporters who exposed him,' Harry laughed raucously.

Harry said he had phoned the police and tipped them off about Clarke's hideout but they wouldn't arrest him.

Chuckling, he turned to me and said, 'Then I phoned Shay and he was down here in twenty minutes.'

On the way back, Shay explained that all was not as it seemed. He tried to unravel the plot, revealing that he'd been investigating Harry, who, in turn, had fallen out with his former cronies. Intrigue, ever present.

The following morning, Shay drove to Manila and we spent a leisurely day in the city. The last few days had been busy but the trip was almost over and I settled in for an early night. I needed it.

The phone rang.

It was Roger. Back from Angeles City. He's excited. It's worked. And they got their photographs. It's going to be a big story. A splash. Maybe even the front page.

'I'm bushed. We'll catch up at breakfast,' Roger rasped down the line.

I said goodnight, turned out the light, the tiredness returning.

The phone rang. It was Alistair.

'Can you come down to my room? You're not going to believe this.'

Alistair seemed different somehow. Roger was in a chair looking wasted. A girl, in a black sequinned top and blue jeans, sat cross-legged on the bed. Alistair stumbled through the story, his words tangled up in the rush to get them out.

'Frenzy's a dancer from a go-go bar in Angeles City. I want to save her. I want to buy her out of the club. I want her to go to college.' He said. 'I'm just not this kind of guy. It's crazy. She's not my girlfriend or anything. But I've been thinking about what you said and I really want to help this girl. Can Shay help?'

It's another late night.

If the girl was serious about getting out of the industry, Shay told me he would help, but he'd seen it before.

While most of the girls want to leave, many struggle with the requirements of a life that is so different, and, sadly, very few make it.

At breakfast, there was a confrontation between Roger and Alistair. Roger was annoyed, insisting that the first rule of journalism was not to get involved with 'the story'. Roger insisted, 'You've got to stay detached.'

Roger reviewed his own investigation of the last few days, speculating on the angles that the paper would be interested in. When he heard that I had told the police, in Olongapo, that Bruce Teasdale from Paradise Express had arrived in the Philippines, he decided that Alistair should stay over and try for some photos of his arrest.

In the few hours that remained, I embarked on a shopping expedition. I was taken to the Megamall. Malls are a phenomenon in the Philippines and have taken the country by storm. There's a simple reason why they're so successful: air-conditioning. This mall was the largest in Manila, six floors and as long as an airport runway. It was bewildering, all-encompassing, like a maze. Beyond the ritual of shopping, this had become an experience, and entire families spent the day there. I lasted eleven minutes and then ran for cover in one of the ModestMalls, but I just couldn't commit to purchase anything. Everything seemed … just like, but not exactly. I spotted the recently released *Elvis 50s Masters Box Set*. But here, even the box set looked smaller. I know. I've looked at the set in every country I've visited, waiting for the price to drop.

Roger was in the business section, I was in cattle class. He wanted to upgrade me but the flight was full. I tried to read but just couldn't concentrate. These past five days in the Philippines had been taken at breakneck speed and lived at the edge, but curiously the priorities were clear. I told myself that I didn't want to go back to the same-old-used-to-be, as the song goes. I wanted to remain in pursuit of those things that are important, to be focused on what was essential. Sometimes I felt cluttered with the business of life and the meaning of life had been forgotten, neglected.

As the silver jet soared into the sky, the roads and homes and shacks and parks and fields and hills started to shrink, resembling a grid on a computer game.

I started to doze on the plane, fleeting thoughts coming through the ether on the fragility of life, the passing of time. It's been a late night, again. This time I didn't mind. I was on my way home.

In my mind, I kept replaying vignettes from the past few extraordinary days. Would Clarke get convicted? Would Fitzgerald sail away on his yacht? How would the *News of the World* report the story and would it be sensationalised beyond recognition? Was 747 Travel still operating? Had Stone and Mitchell got away? Was there anything that could be done or should I just forget about it?

Like a movie that started at the end and played itself backward, the days of my life premiered on a video screen in my mind, and the past unfolded.

Yesterday. Last week. Last month. Last year.

Sometimes I felt like an actor who had stumbled on to the wrong stage. How did I get here?

4

I Had No Idea. Abbey Wood 1981

Was it chance, design or, as Bob Dylan puts it, just a simple twist of fate?

In 1981, the map of the future looked clear.

At *Rolling Stone's* Fifth Avenue office in New York City, a senior editor was enthusiastic about developing a book about my good friend, Mike Porco, the owner of the legendary 'Gerde's Folk City' in Greenwich Village. Virtually everyone in the business had played Folk City and Mike had a story about nearly everyone. The book was a winner and I knew it.

Mike became legal guardian to a young wannabe in 1961, fed him roast beef sandwiches, lent him a shirt, paid for his publicity photos and booked him to play his first paying gig at the club. *New York Times* music critic, Robert Shelton, was impressed and his review helped land a recording contract for the young folk singer. Bob Dylan's career was on the road.

Dylan never forgot Mike. Two decades later, Dylan threw a surprise birthday party for Mike at Folk City and was joined onstage by an all star cast. This impromptu concert led to the Rolling Thunder Revue, a free-wheeling, rambling tour that provided the visual backdrop for Dylan's four-hour film, *Renaldo and Clara*.

When another American publisher waved a contract in front of me for a book about Bob Dylan (with whom I'd had a brief encounter while in Los Angeles), it was like a neon sign lighting up the road ahead. My career was moving ahead but my private life seemed to be disintegrating just as fast. I was developing outlines, assembling chapter structures and transcribing tapes for both books, when the telephone rang. It was Peter Meadows, an entrepreneurial visionary character, with a reputation for talking tough but getting things done.

'*Buzz* magazine is launching a new project at Spring Harvest,' Peter said. 'Are you interested in working on it?' Peter outlined the story of an obscure group called the Siberian Seven, in Moscow.

Human rights had been a passing interest. I'd stood in the rain at a vigil outside the Soviet Embassy for imprisoned writer Vladimir Bukovsky, and attended protests by 'The 35's' (the Women's Campaign for Soviet Jewry). I'd also joined Robert Shelton and another writer, Liz Thompson, in launching Joan Baez's human rights group, Humanitas, in Britain.

My conditions were simple.

'Three and a half days a week, with the option of working from home, strictly for two months,' I replied. 'And £500 a month.'

I didn't think Peter would go for it, but after a pause, he said, 'Can you start on Monday?'

It seemed relatively easy money and I didn't think an occasional visit to the magazine's South London office would prove too much of a distraction.

I had no idea.

5

Siberian Protest 1963-1978

The Bolshevik revolution in 1917 in Russia led to a relentless war against the Christian faith over the subsequent decades. The Russian Orthodox Church was legally dissolved and a controlled group established in its place. More than twelve thousand clergy were murdered, and over one hundred thousand lay leaders killed. The majority were shot. Some were beaten, more were hanged. Others were drowned. By 1939, the number of Orthodox parish churches had been forcibly reduced from fifty-four thousand to less than one hundred, while a few 'show churches' remained opened.

President Nikita Khrushchev continued the assault in the fifties and promised to wipe out Christianity. The last Christian, he thundered, would become a relic to be ridiculed on public television. The Twenty-Second Congress of the Communist Party of the Soviet Union launched a detailed programme to establish a communist society without religion. One of the first steps taken was to register all churches. Registration handed control over to the state, and those who refused to comply were considered outlaws and became targets for the authorities. The crackdown intensified. Widespread arrests followed as churches were attacked, leaders hunted down and thousands of believers jailed.

The Soviet machine was now in gear, sweeping away every religious icon and image in its path. Nowhere was this rage greater than in Chernogorsk, a small, coal-mining town in Siberia. The Christians in this remote community took a dramatic and historic decision and decided to organise the first demonstration ever held inside the USSR. Secretly, thirty-two Siberians travelled the two thousand miles to Moscow and burst into the American Embassy on January 3 1963. Their intention was to appeal for help from the Americans and to trumpet their plight to the rest of the world.

Their demonstration in 1963 created a sensation as the story hit the front pages in the west. The Christians from Siberia had burst on to the centre stage and turned the spotlight on themselves. It was the first indication that Christianity had survived communism's brutal offensive.

British author John Pollock was commissioned by Hodder & Stoughton publishers to travel to Russia to investigate the incident and to track down these protesters. He never met anyone from Chernogorsk and all he could do was come up with the name of the leader: Vashchenko.

Pollock's book, *The Christians from Siberia,* included a chapter on the protest and was the first publication to deal with the survival of the Christian faith after half a century of militant atheistic rule. Fifteen years later, in 1978, a Christian couple working at the American Embassy in Moscow were reading Pollock's book and recognised the Vashchenko name. They were in for a surprise.

Peter Vashchenko and seven others had returned to the American Embassy in 1978, to seek advice about emigrating. When a Soviet guard at the gate stopped Peter's sixteen year old son and wrestled him to the ground, the others dashed inside. Initially, they wanted help in rescuing John but the American officials were reluctant to get involved. The Siberian families expected the Americans to be sympathetic to their reports of persecution and harassment. Instead, the US exercised a 'get tough' policy and pressured the group to leave the building.

The Siberians had reason to fear reprisals from the Soviet authorities. Each of them had direct experience of the brutality and terror tactics of the Soviet secret police.

Peter Vashchenko and his wife Augustina had both been imprisoned for their beliefs, once at the same time, despite having young children at home. Lida and Lyuba, their daughters, had been forcibly removed from their home to be interned in a re-education institute.

Timothy Chmykhalov, one of the Siberian Seven and just sixteen in 1978, was a young child when police raided his home searching for religious literature. He watched his father and other family members dragged off and jailed.

Millions of families throughout the country shared the experiences of the Siberian Seven. Theirs was a story of courage and determined hope in the face of heart-wrenching torment and psychological terror. Their crime was simply to be practising Christians and to want to raise their children in the faith.

The Siberians lived in daily fear of being evicted from the lobby of the American Embassy and faced many tense deadlines. Somehow, the Americans always pulled back at the last moment before forcing them out. They were ignored, treated like outcasts and forced to stand in a corner of the waiting room, sleeping in their clothes. Concerned that they were attracting attention from Embassy visitors, they were moved to a tiny, claustrophobic basement room, about twenty foot by fifteen, remote and out of bounds; sympathetic staff took them food.

Convinced that if they left the Embassy's territory, no one would ever see them again, the Siberians endured the hostility and intimidation of their reluctant hosts. The Americans were concerned that if they were seen to be helping this group, their Embassy would be deluged with similar protests and appeals. They probably assumed that the enforced isolation of the Siberians would result in the Seven leaving the building in despair.

The deadlock intensified with each passing day.

The Christian couple who were reading Pollock's book were amazed to learn that the same people that the British author had pursued a decade ago – the Vashchenkos – were back, a decade later, and now lived like naughty school children in the Embassy's basement. Their support at such a crucial time in 1978 could well have played an important role in stopping US officials from finally evicting the Seven from the building. The couple arranged a visit for the renowned British author finally to meet the Christians from Siberia and a book was rushed out, hoping that the publicity might help their case.

Pollock called his book *The Siberian Seven*.

Privately, American diplomats warned that the Siberians' case would never be resolved. 'Someday, they're going to have to walk out of the Embassy or be carried out. That's all.'

A hard wooden bench marked the borderline of their basement refuge. East led to the courtyard and the gate with the Soviet guards. Westward, some footsteps away, was a repair shop, the building's power generator, and beyond this, a dingy passageway. Here a random assortment of broken and unwanted chattels and possessions had been dumped: smashed television sets gathering dust, faded magazines bound with twine, slide projectors in need of repair, Hoovers rusting in the corner…

Amidst the debris, broken and rejected junk, seven people had been discarded, and now they waited, watching the corridor, watching the window, watching the wheels turn. Writing letters, thinking of family back home in Siberia, grandchildren they hadn't seen. Watching the Soviet guards, silently hearing their threats and curses. Watching the single window in their room, and, at night, watching the stars.

Basement Encounter 1981

Peter Meadows launched the Campaign to Free the Siberian Seven at Spring Harvest in April 1981 and thousands signed a twenty-two foot long petition in support. His next ambitious idea was to hold a rally in Trafalgar Square to publicise the case. Ten days before the event, I had an idea about the best way to get media coverage and suggested that Peter should go to Moscow and capture the scoop – the first interview with the Seven.

Peter recognised its news value. 'I'm too busy,' he said emphatically, but with a lazy grin, added, 'What are you doing this weekend?'

When I told our travel agent that I had plans for the weekend, she laughed out loud. 'You can't fly to Moscow and get back in time for your meeting at Trafalgar Square. We need ten to fifteen working days for a visa.'

She explained the 'Catch-22' situation regarding travel to the Soviet Union. You couldn't book a ticket without a visa and you could only apply for a visa if you had a ticket. It seemed a conspiracy between airline and consular staff to make travel to the USSR as difficult as possible.

Our demonstration in Trafalgar Square was scheduled for 27 June 1981. There just weren't enough days to get a visa, fly to Moscow, and to return in time for the meeting.

That evening, I finally reached David Willis, a foreign correspondent in Moscow when the saga started. He was brilliant and helped piece together some of the puzzles in the story. I told him that I wanted to go to Moscow but couldn't get a visa. David drawled, 'There's only one person who can get you a visa in a few days. His name's Barry Martin. He could be anywhere in the world. You'll probably never reach him but here's his telephone number.'

I hung up and dialled the number. It rang three times and a husky voice answered, 'Barry Martin.'

I didn't know who he was but told him everything. 'Will you help me?'

Barry asked a few questions and then there was a long pause. The waiting was excruciating.

'Be at my office near Oxford Street at 7.30am tomorrow morning. Bring your passport and four photographs – for your visa – with you.'

Within a few days, I had my visa and a ticket to Moscow.

Barry Martin had emerged like an angel from nowhere, making the impossible possible.

There was no time to prepare. There were just things to do. Nothing more important than making arrangements to feed my black cat, Durango Rolling Thunder, while I was on assignment in Moscow.

The Americans had declared the Siberian Seven's basement room off limits and no one was permitted to cross that line, but before leaving London, I'd been given the name of an Embassy official who was sympathetic to their plight and might help. I had flown to Moscow, willing to take that chance.

'Come on down,' my contact said, on the telephone.

Moscow taxi drivers broke all the rules and created some new ones. Rusty Skodas raced through red lights, sending innocent pedestrians scurrying to the pavement. Capitalistic concepts were alive and well in the communist capital. A taxi journey from my hotel to the American Embassy on Chaikovskova Street varied from one to ten roubles, depending on the route. Frequently, I got the grand tour.

Twenty minutes later I was at the American Embassy gates, waving my passport at the Russian guards, and walking through, as though this was part of my normal routine. Inside the courtyard, I quickly located the appropriate entry point and found the passage that led to the lift. The lift had just one button. It stopped on just one floor. His floor. My contact was a senior military official, probably a CIA spook.

George Powell greeted me with a firm handshake and after a few minutes inside his nondescript office we went back to the one-stop lift for a walk outside. George was sympathetic. 'I'd like to help but I doubt if you'd get official permission to see them. No one else has.'

We walked on in silence, then George said mysteriously, 'There may be another way.'

George sketched the layout of the building on my notepad and pinpointed the basement room. 'The rest is up to you,' he grinned, 'Of course, I've never seen this paper before.'

George pointed out men who he claimed were KGB agents and as we walked, someone in a black leather jacket approached us and said to me, 'English.' It was a statement, rather than a question. Not waiting for confirmation, his face grimaced, he gripped his chest as if he'd been shot, and in a tortured voice, exclaimed,

'John Lennon!' Without another word, he straightened up, and walked on as though nothing had happened.

Before we returned to the Embassy, George explained that he regularly debriefed 'couriers' during walks like ours and expected our stroll in the sun to have been monitored. 'The KGB may assume that you have brought some hot news for me,' he cautioned. 'Be careful. After all, we're in the midst of a cold war.' He shook my hand and disappeared into one of the side doors.

The directions were precise. A dark winding corridor, a barber shop, and finally, the basement room, with its door that could never be closed.

The Siberians were unprepared for my sudden arrival but within a short time, I was welcomed within their circle as a friend and shared moments that have become unforgettable memories.

The Siberian Seven's basement window in the American Embassy in Moscow.

Photo: Danny Smith

The Siberian Seven were described by the authorities as peasant Pentecostals, possibly fanatics, who thought that if they stayed in the Embassy long enough, the benign Americans would take pity and unlock their door to freedom. Simple people who had simply misunderstood and were now pawns on the chessboard of the super powers. Nothing could be further from the truth. In fact, Peter Vashchenko had developed an effective strategy, having been closely involved with the first demonstration ever held inside the USSR, in 1963. Those tactics were subsequently used effectively by the human rights movement, who understood that publicity offered the best protection.

Peter's daughter, Lyuba, aged twenty-eight, had taught herself English and translated for visitors who stumbled into their sanctuary. Lida, their eldest daughter, was perceptive and subtle. At one point, Lyuba told

The Vashchenko family, left to right, back row: Lyuba, Augustina and Peter; front row,: Lida and Lilya.
Photo: Danny Smith

me that for a long time no one knew of their situation. 'No one at all,' Lyuba emphasised her words. Lida mumbled something causing Lyuba to chuckle. Shyly, she explained, 'Lida said, "You're wrong when you said that no one knew about us. Someone did know."' The implication was obvious and did not require amplification.

The Vashchenko's youngest daughter, Lilya, aged twenty-four, was simply charming. In another context, she would have young men leaving flowers at her door.

'See, not everyone dislikes us,' Lilya said and pointed to Erica, the stray cat that had taken up residence in the basement with them. More recently, a kitten had followed Erica into the room and proved a playful distraction.

'You must name the kitten before you leave,' Lida insisted.

'That's a serious business,' I replied.

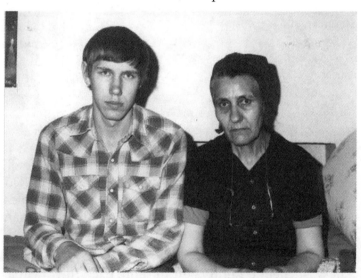

Timothy and his mother, Maria Chmykhalov, shared the basement room.   Photo: Danny Smith

Maria Chmykhalov and her young son, Timothy, shared this space and, at times, things were tense between the families. Maria divided her time between knitting, writing letters home and reading the Scriptures.

But any smiles faded quickly as a simple distraction reminded them of family, friends, and home, far, far away.

Over the next few days, my time was spent visiting foreign correspondents, introducing the Campaign in London. It was our intention to revive the story, suggesting that after three years living as 'hostages of conscience', the Siberian Seven deserved coverage.

Most of the foreign correspondents were sympathetic, but there were exceptions. The first journalist I rang snarled, 'No, I'm not interested in that story,' and slammed the phone down. Andrew Nagorsky, from *Newsweek*, was curious. He'd recently arrived in Moscow and, unaware of the drama at the Embassy, asked lots of questions. Nigel Wade, from the *Daily Telegraph*, was enthusiastic. 'Third anniversary? No, I didn't realise that. Yes, come on down.' Michael Binyon from *The Times* invited me to his high rise apartment and talked about the phenomenon of reporting from inside a censorship machine. 'It's like living on another planet,' he enthused. When I asked if he wanted to leave, his reply was instant and emphatic, 'Gosh, no, there's nowhere else I'd rather be.'

Barry Martin had booked me into the National Hotel, a large, ornate, old style rambling building just off Red Square. I returned to the hotel that evening and minutes later there was a knock on the door. A tough young man in a short black leather jacket thrust a note into my hand, swaggered down the corridor, and entered the room adjacent to mine. The note was from a journalist from Associated Press: 'Call me,' it said.

As I stepped from the shower, the telephone rang.

'Mr Smith? Are you OK? Everything OK?'

'Yes,' I replied. 'Who is this?'

The caller remained silent and then hung up. Ten minutes later, the phone rang again. No one spoke, though I could hear papers rustling and someone walking around. The sounds on the telephone appeared to replicate what I could hear next door.

I opened a window. The fresh air felt good. I decided to explore the city. The buildings were drab, cold, grey concrete blocks of stone, assembled at random. The people seemed preoccupied, morose, their eyes distant; they caught your gaze and then looked away. Cars raced past, horns blaring. Stragglers scurried for the pavement. I strolled on, oblivious to everything around me, walking without purpose, following my feet.

Within five minutes, two men had accosted me in separate incidents. Both were dressed remarkably sim-ilarly, in a kind of standard issue black leather jacket, and both appeared to have information about me. I dismissed these chance encounters and brushed aside the second man like a pet dog.

Back at the National I was confronted with the bad news that I'd missed dinner. It took skill, ingenuity – and some foreign currency – to secure the promise of food.

When dinner was served, I was dismayed. The fried egg was stuck to the plate and had to be scraped off. Several minutes later, the butter arrived, made up of numerous small, individual pieces. It looked as if the leftovers from everyone else's plate had been dumped on mine.

Still hungry, I left the dining room in search of food and stumbled into the bar. 'Dollars! Dollars!' came the command when I tried to buy chocolates with a £5 note. Sensing my distress, a friendly barman came to the rescue and a deal was struck.

The bar was a large, dimly lit room with high ceilings and a gloomy atmosphere. Within minutes, two young Russian girls appeared at my table. They were curiously well informed about my trip, while their questions seemed rehearsed. Juliet pressed herself against me and whispered details about the pleasures I could expect if I would accompany them to 'some other place close by.'

Seated nearby were members of a British film crew, and Andy, the sound technician, told me that Moscow was 'unbelievable'. I nodded knowingly. At another table, a group of businessmen fawned over a strikingly attractive girl with a voluptuous figure wearing a scarlet dress the size of a handkerchief. She was a film star shooting a movie in Moscow.

The man from the room next to mine sauntered into the bar, collected a bottle and left. He was only in the room for a few minutes but the staff seemed nervous when they spoke to him.

I was at the bar when I felt someone behind me and then a hand on my wrist. It was the film star in the scarlet handkerchief.

'I know you,' she pouted, speaking with a harsh Russian accent. 'You born in India but you travel with Irish passport. Why you do that?'

She spoke her words like a fortune teller at a country fairground. There wasn't any build up, no sense of mystery, no tantalising clue, but her words gripped me with the kind of shock and suspense on which Alfred Hitchcock had built his legendary career. Although the other strangers I had encountered hinted with casual, ironic remarks, this was undoubtedly someone who had access to information about me.

I extricated myself from the girl with the movie star looks and found Juliet waiting. She launched a final offensive to entice me out of the hotel, but accepted defeat with a compromise. 'At least, telephone me,' she pouted, and scribbled her number in my note book.

That night I was awoken around 3am by the telephone. No one spoke and there was an eerie silence at the end of the line. The hotel was quiet but I could hear someone moving around next door. I checked that my door was bolted and pulled on my clothes and shoes. Somehow it gave me confidence, though, strangely, I didn't feel afraid.

I checked my airline ticket at breakfast. Just one more day in Moscow. I pictured myself en route to Paris and then on to Heathrow.

In the hotel's lobby, the British television crew were assembling their equipment. Andy was nursing a hangover and when I told him about the phone calls and encounters, he looked incomprehensibly at me. 'Really,' he said, slightly dazed.

Sensing that the conversation was going nowhere, I decided it was time to start knocking on the media's door. It was clear that if I didn't contact the correspondents, the story wouldn't be reported and I was determined to make every moment count. I had worked the media relentlessly but there were still people on the list: Walter Wisniewski, UPI; Serge Schmenen, *New York Times*; Gordon Joseloff, CBS; John Morrison, Reuters…

Sometime in the afternoon, I made it to John Osman's apartment. The BBC's veteran reporter was brilliant. With a Campaign in Britain, he had a hook for the story and he scribbled notes as we talked.

Before leaving, I told him of my experiences, starting with the meeting with the US intelligence official. He asked a few pertinent questions, and then said, 'Hm. It sounds like they're on to you. I suspect they're going to pick you up.'

'What do you mean? Arrest me?' I was astonished. This had never occurred to me.

'Probably,' John replied. 'If so, I'll broadcast your arrest on the radio, reveal why you've come to Moscow and explain that you're not a spy.'

He had moved swiftly into gear. It had become another story and he knew exactly what to do.

But I was quiet as the seriousness of the situation hit me.

John explained that the surveillance, obvious in the extreme, was meant to intimidate me. 'They want you to know that they're watching you.'

'I don't know what to do next,' I mumbled.

'Just carry on as usual,' John advised. 'But I'll help. I know the procedure. I know what to do. I'll come and get you out of prison.'

John had an idea. He arranged for me to telephone him at regular intervals. 'This is serious,' he said sternly. 'You must call me wherever you are. If you haven't called, I'll assume you've been arrested and I'll set the wheels in motion. I want to broadcast the news within an hour of your arrest. It's important.'

Outside, everything seemed calm, normal. Across the street, two men sat in a black car parked at the curb. Were they plain clothes waiting to grab me and bundle me into the boot? Would they pull me off the street in broad daylight? Why were this couple staring at me from the corner? Was the empty taxi that cruised past a decoy?

It was like a movie.

I chased after the taxi and jumped in, directing him to Chaikovskovo Street and the Embassy building. I thought it would be my final chance to see the Siberian Seven.

One last goodbye.

On the Run

Peter Vashchenko sounded alarmed. He was convinced that the surveillance was a direct consequence of the contact with the American intelligence officer and my time spent in the basement with them. I had become a target.

He told me about a recent shooting between British and Russian agents in Switzerland. It was a tangled tale that had received meagre coverage but, according to Peter, the Russians wanted revenge. 'It's very dangerous for you,' he warned. 'They could make you disappear – just like that!' He snapped his fingers, as Lyuba interpreted his words.

'Just like they did with Raoul Wallenberg,' Lida continued. Wallenberg was the Swedish diplomat who rescued Jews from Hitler's concentration camps but then disappeared, and 'died', inside Russia, though there were persistent rumours that he was still alive.

A heated debate broke out between Peter and Lida. 'He's in the west,' Peter declared authoritatively.

'But how can you be sure?' Lida argued.

'The west would never have abandoned him,' Peter shook his head vehemently.

In the tiny basement room, with daylight slowly fading, their hushed voices chronicled accounts of spies and surveillance; some were dramatic, many were personal. They claimed that there were over twenty listening devices or bugs in their room, and were convinced that many of the Russian staff at the Embassy spied on the Americans.

The Americans had relented and recently allowed them outside the room for an hour each day. Maria Chmykhalov pulled a mauve patterned shawl around her shoulders and headed for the door, as the others followed.

Alone in the room, I fidgeted, and then a brilliant idea for an unusual photograph sent me in search of them. A photo of the Seven outside had to be interesting. The courtyard at the back was a fairly large area. I saw the Seven at the far end and walked towards them.

Lyuba spotted me first. I could tell she was annoyed. Her eyes made signals my mind couldn't read.

I handed my Pentax ME Super to Timothy and outlined some suggestions for the photos. 'With the Embassy as the backdrop,' I instructed him.

I crossed the courtyard to check out some options. I was enjoying playing art director, and wondered what kind of set up Annie Leibovitz would select if she were here. We'd have to move quickly because the light was fading.

'Excuse me, sir,' someone called out. 'Can I help you?'

'No, it's fine,' I replied, jauntily. I was having fun and didn't need anyone meddling, particularly some amateur.

The marine identified himself as security. 'Are you visiting someone in the Embassy, sir?'

'Yes,' I replied, nonchalantly, 'I'm visiting the Vashchenko and Chmykhalov families.'

His demeanour changed rapidly. 'The Siberians!' He virtually spat the words out. 'You haven't been in the basement, have you?' he charged.

Still oblivious to the danger, I sailed in, 'Yes, I've been into the room to see them.'

'Did you realise that's a restricted area?' His tone turned aggressive.

'No, I didn't,' I said, casually. This was the American Embassy and he was a marine. He wasn't the KGB.

He stared intently at me and then stated, 'I'm going to ask you to leave these premises immediately. You are not to have any further contact with the Siberians. You must not return here. Do you understand me? Sir!'

It felt as though I had been struck. Stung, I stared incomprehensibly at him as his words hung in the air.

'Do you understand me?' his voice lowered in tone as he inched closer toward me.

'Yes,' I answered, clearly shocked. 'But I've got to say goodbye to my friends.'

'Permission refused.' The marine and I were almost touching. 'You must leave immediately.'

'But that's ridiculous,' I protested. 'My passport, coat, money – everything I have is still in their room.' I couldn't disguise the frustration in my voice.

The marine and I had reached an impasse. Finally he broke the silence. 'Collect your things, and leave immediately.' He was emphatic. 'Don't return.'

I expected someone to step from the shadows and go 'Joke!' But no one did.

My throat was dry and I felt slightly dizzy. Each step seemed to require great effort. It felt as though I was walking under water. There was an irony here, I knew it, but it was hard to focus. Someone was writing a message in the sand, but before I could read it, the tide flowed in and washed the words away.

The KGB had mistaken me for a spy because of my links with the US Embassy and now I was on the wanted list of the Russian secret police. But the Americans were treating me like a criminal, evicting me from the one place that I thought I'd be safe, forcing me out into the streets and into the arms of the KGB.

How had things got so tangled, and who could help me now? I had John Osman's telephone number but what could he do? There was just no one to turn to. I was alone, a target for both the KGB and the Americans.

It was dusk with a low smoky light that bathed the courtyard in a dull glow.

I whispered a prayer and walked quietly back into the Embassy building to see the Siberians. They had left the courtyard during the encounter with the marine and looked downcast and forlorn as I explained what had happened.

'But where will you go? It's not safe for you in Moscow.' Lyuba had articulated the obvious. Night was almost on us, and I wasn't desperate to return to the streets of Moscow or to my room at the National. Neither did I want to burden the Seven with my problems.

Peter Vashchenko took charge, as Lyuba interpreted his words. 'It's dangerous for you to be on your own. You will stay with us tonight.'

It was an electrifying moment. Words were spoken in hushed whispers, as the room seemed charged with the tensions of the night.

'My greatest fear is that the Americans will take revenge and punish you,' I said, speaking as softly as I could, in a muffled voice, to the others who had huddled round.

'My greatest fear is that the Russians will take revenge and punish you,' Peter retorted, brushing aside my protests.

It had been an extraordinary day. Just when I assumed that there was no shelter and no hope, help had come, beyond anything that I could have expected at a risk none of us could afford. People with nothing had offered everything they had.

The suspense was intensifying. When would the marine come to check that I had obeyed his instructions and had left the room? How would this tiny cramped room accommodate me when it was too small for them? Who else would walk into this room and find me here – this room with a door that could never be closed? And what punishment would the Americans heap on the Seven if they discovered what they had done?

Timothy and Lilya kept a look-out, watching from the corridor. If anyone approached, I was to go into the bathroom with one of the girls, who would pretend to take a shower.

Would it work? Who could tell?

There was another problem. Every evening, the marine on guard duty checked on them, and he walked through the room.

'What time does he usually come?' My voice was raised in anxiety as I considered this new hazard.

Lida's finger pressed against her lips. 'Shhhh.' She conveyed a gentle assertiveness. Silence. Secret. 'He could come at any time but usually it's late.'

'Come, eat,' Augustina smiled, handing me a plate of delicious fried chicken. Few words were spoken as the evening chores were completed. Just as we were finishing dinner, footsteps could be heard in the corridor. I moved swiftly into the bathroom, in line with our plan. Ten minutes later, Timothy tapped the all-clear signal on the door.

The next hour would be decisive but Augustina suggested that we get to bed early to minimise the risk.

Chairs and boxes were moved, sleeping bags unrolled as Peter and Timothy worked quickly. 'This is where you will sleep. No one will find you here even if they entered the room,' Peter spoke with authority.

I didn't think it possible, but, astonishingly, in their tiny cramped room they exercised an act of creative genius. Where seven people already slept, space had been found, but not just space, an actual hiding place had emerged.

The table against the wall was pulled back slightly to allow space between it and the wall. Then cardboard boxes, clothes, books were piled up around the legs of the table. In the hollow, a crawl space had been created. Timothy tried it out. It was true. You couldn't tell that a body was there.

And for one single night, I joined them and we became 'the Siberian Eight.' This incident would remain our secret, never revealed till now.

One final act before bedtime.

With the door wide open, we knelt on the cold floor, in the centre of the room, as scriptures were read, voices raised in prayer. I've never known a moment of such vulnerability or such power.

I crawled into position behind the table, as Peter and Timothy moved the boxes over me, adjusting them slightly.

'It's perfect,' Peter smiled, as he knelt on the floor beside me. 'God has given us the power to keep you safe.'

The room had offered up a hiding place and in return I sheltered in its secret.

Maria slept on one bed, Peter and Augustina on the other. Space was cleared in the middle of the room, where three girls spread makeshift mattresses on the floor. Timothy slept in the corridor.

I lay in darkness on an old sleeping bag, listening to the movement in the room. When sleep came, I journeyed along its highway like a hitchhiker in need of a ride. Ironically, I slept soundly. When Timothy woke me the following morning, the operation to return the room to its normal state was undertaken swiftly and in silence.

We said goodbye in the dimly lit hall just outside the basement room. Each one clasped my hands, whispering words of encouragement. I couldn't think. My words seemed frozen. 'I'll never forget you,' was all that I could mumble.

I walked out of the Embassy unnoticed and headed straight for the National. No sound came from the room next to mine, though the door was ajar. I threw my clothes into the suitcase and checked out of the hotel. With hours to spare before my flight, I didn't want to spend an extra minute in Moscow and headed for the safety of the airport.

But there was to be one final twist.

At the deserted airport lounge, I was distracted for a few minutes while paying a bill for a drink and left my hand luggage unattended. Unnoticed, two young men appeared nearby for a few minutes and then left. Twenty-four hours later, back in London, I learned that all the film that had been carried in my cloth bag had been ruined; some was missing, other films had been exposed. The only film that could be developed was from a roll that I carried in my waistcoat. It was mystifying.

All the way back I was haunted by that basement encounter. Not a depression, but a sadness. I was on a flight to London, changing planes in Paris. Back to family, friends, home.

In a way that was hard to explain, the encounter in Moscow rekindled a spark of faith within me. Spirituality, I suspected, had more to do with attitudes of the heart, a way of being, our response to situations, and was far removed from the marketing system that produced an off-the-shelf, easy-to-slip-into religious experience.

Inexplicably, I felt myself warmed by the encounter in Moscow and sensed a determination within to rediscover personal priorities in my pursuit of God. The tables turned, my offerings of help seemed feeble and hollow. All other projects slid and faded. In Moscow, I had made seven new friends with the pain of their situation all too real. Nothing else seemed important.

My beliefs had never been tested, nor my convictions challenged. Perhaps it was meeting people who were paying a terrible price for a belief that I took casually. Perhaps Moscow found me on holiday from my convictions, or maybe Moscow held up a mirror and I saw myself for the first time as I really was and not the façade that I had constructed. Someone adrift, taking refuge in transitory pursuits, gaining comfort from inconsequential concerns, fooling others, but ultimately fooling only myself.

I didn't understand nor did I want to explain why I was feeling the way I did. I just wanted that moment to remain and to be changed by its power. If I was searching for a cause, I didn't know it. In a curious way, I felt like an explorer who had wandered far off course and suddenly recognised the trail leading out of the forest. I thought I had lost my life, now it seemed as though it was being returned to me.

But what would I do? What could I do?

I just had no idea.

6

The Campaign To Free the Siberian Seven

Moscow was an extraordinary experience and I returned shell-shocked and dazed. But there was hardly time to think, to order my thoughts. Peter Meadows' flair for capturing attention was at work. With the media alerted, photographs were processed overnight. They were the first photographs of the Siberians in three years and copies were biked to newspaper offices all over the city.

The press conference was packed. Reporters from television, radio and the nationals were all there. Even my friend, Robert Shelton, who had moved from New York City to Brighton, sat at the back, observing the scene. 'This is quite a story,' he remarked, giving me a hug.

* * * *

Peter Meadows' brilliant idea had caught the media's attention: a live telephone link to the Siberians in Moscow.

The Seven had recently been granted one telephone call a month, mainly used by their prime US supporter, Jane Drake, a housewife in Little Rock. Jane agreed that we could use her telephone allocation for June and the phone link was made. We knew that the Americans would be furious when they realised that the media were listening in on our conversation but the Siberians agreed that it was worth taking the risk. The telephone call lasted about twelve minutes and Lyuba handled it brilliantly.

Gavin Scott of BBC TV's *Newsnight* asked her, 'What will happen to you when the American Embassy shifts to another building next year? Are you worried?'

'We don't know what's going to happen to us from day to day, how can we think about next year?' Lyuba answered, somewhat bemused.

Peter Sissons reported the event on ITV's lunchtime news; *Newsnight* devoted eight minutes to the launch of

The phone call: John Pollock, second left, Danny Smith and Canon Michael Bourdeaux, of Keston College, far right   Photo: Chris Gander

the Campaign to Free the Siberian Seven; the *Daily Mail* headlined, 'The People the West Forgot' and radio stations across the country broadcast extracts from the telephone call.

That Saturday, the media coverage was outstanding, as BBC TV news filed regular reports. Following Peter Meadows's successful promotion at Spring Harvest, three thousand people attended our rally at Trafalgar Square and marched to the Soviet Embassy in Kensington, accompanied by television cameras.

The Siberian Seven's third anniversary, on 27 June, may have been dismal in Moscow but in London and beyond, they were making television news for the first time ever.

The Campaign's launch had been successful, concluding the terms of my 'assignment'. But this part-time job was turning into a full-time obsession.

Thousands of people supported the meeting at Trafalgar Square. Photo: Chris Gander

At the end of the telephone call at the press conference, I reminded Lyuba that Lida had asked me to name her kitten. 'I'd like you to call the kitten "Star". We watch and are watched by the same stars. It will also remind you that there are people who will not forget you and will work for your freedom.'

The Siberians were people I knew and cared for. They were in trouble, and I felt I had to do everything I could to help them. It was simply a commitment to a group of friends. I could never forget their help for me. The experience in Moscow would remain our secret, hidden from everyone.

One week after the Trafalgar Square march, we recorded a half hour television documentary for ATV in Birmingham and the reporter's final question stung me,

Just back from Moscow in time for the Trafalgar Square demonstration.   Photo: Mick Rock

'Will the Siberian Seven ever be free? What's your personal opinion?'

I had never thought of the question until that moment. I knew that I wanted to dedicate myself and everything that I had to work for their freedom. 'Not only do I believe that they will be free but I will not stop until that dream has turned into a reality.' I was surprised by the confidence in my voice. It was more than theatrics. My words articulated and reinforced an inner feeling and my answer was not spoken primarily to the television audience. It was a message to myself. The response came from my heart and I never wavered from that conviction.

Driving back to London from the Birmingham television interview with Peter Meadows, I assured him that my reply to the reporter's question wasn't hype and we started brainstorming ways of maintaining the momentum of the Campaign.

Peter Vashchenko's birthday was next. Could we set up a mobile birthday party? Give out birthday cake to politicians, newspaper editors and everyone else on Fleet Street? The cake could be accompanied by invitation cards from our absent host. The last stop would be at the Soviet Embassy requesting the Ambassador's assistance in resolving this issue. We could ask supporters around the country to hold their own 'birthday celebrations'. Maybe Bryce Cooke at Piccadilly Radio would turn his programme into a party? Who could we get to distribute the cake? We knew we wanted press coverage. Hm. What about pretty girls in Siberian frocks? Who could resist such an offer?

By the time we saw the motorway signs for London, the ideas were already taking shape. Peter Vashchenko's birthday was on 30 October. Just three months away. We had a party to organise.

Happy Birthday, Peter Vashchenko!

The Campaign promoted by Spring Harvest and *Buzz* magazine captured the imagination of people throughout the country.

The birthday party was a lorry decorated with a large colourful cardboard cake, balloons, streamers and lovely girls in bright Russian-style costumes giving out cake with a party invitation explaining why the subject, Peter Vashchenko, couldn't attend his own birthday celebrations. Visually, it looked great. Margaret Rigal, one of the founders of the Women's Campaign for Soviet Jewry, was our special party guest and sang along with us to Stevie Wonder's *Happy Birthday*. The song had been written to campaign for a national holiday on Martin Luther King's birthday in the US.

The media loved the mobile birthday party. Everyone took a slice of cake to mark Peter Vashchenko's birthday – only the Soviet Ambassador refused.

Photo: Mick Rock

Television cameras recorded Joan Edgar, one of the 'party girls', with me as we handed out cake to newspaper editors along Fleet Street. The colourful birthday float cruised down the Strand to Downing Street and the Houses of Parliament, where many MPs and staff accepted a piece of cake. Only the Soviet Ambassador wouldn't come to our party. The media were on hand to record his refusal.

The media coverage was tremendous and everyone left the event on a high. But when I got home to Abbey Wood, there was a surprise waiting. My front door had been smashed in and there were pieces of glass in the hallway; one piece had cut the ear of my cat. The neighbours had heard some disturbance but it remained an unsolved mystery.

Tactically, the 'birthday party' concept formed the template for the Campaign, as we sought visual and inventive ways of communicating our message.

* * * *

My first meeting at the Foreign Office was instructive as three diplomats welcomed me with coffee and smiles. First, I was told that our Campaign had been the most successful of its kind, based on the number of letters they had received. Then they asked me to get our supporters to stop writing to the FO as there was nothing they could do. Taken in by their apparent affability, I expressed concern over US attitudes towards the Seven. One FO official erupted in fury. He slammed the table and yelled, 'Don't you think the Americans are doing everything they can for these people?'

I was overwhelmed by my first encounter in Whitehall and couldn't muster much of a response. The diplomats patted me on the back, told me once again that I was doing a wonderful job, and ushered me into the courtyard at King Charles Street.

There was a cool breeze outside and I found myself walking down Whitehall getting angrier by the minute, as I re-lived the meeting. I vowed that it would be the last time that I would be intimidated by politicians or taken in by the curious code that they use to communicate.

David Alton, the first MP we contacted, arranged another meeting with Lord Trefgarne, but through the wall of words it was evident that Britain would not get involved. It was for the Americans and Russians to resolve. It was SEP; Someone Else's Problem.

The politicians' position gave our Campaign a specific objective: to change the mind of the diplomats, a formidable task. After returning from Moscow, I wrote hundreds of letters asking for help. Anyone. Anywhere. It was like putting a message in a bottle and sailing it out with a prayer.

*   *   *   *

Betsy Ramsey, a human rights activist, telephoned from Sweden. After concluding her business at a pre-arranged meeting with Tore Nilsson, a Member of Parliament, that same day, she had shown him my letter and asked if anything could be done.

'That's just the kind of case I was looking for,' Mr Nilsson asserted.

On Mr Nilsson's desk was a speech he intended to deliver that afternoon in Parliament. He took a pen from the drawer and scribbled the words 'Siberian Seven' in the margin. A few weeks earlier, a Soviet submarine had been captured in Swedish waters and held on suspicion of espionage. Mr Nilsson argued that the Swedish

Government should demand something in return and not merely hand back the vessel to the Soviets.

It was a slender lead but I grabbed it.

I flew to Stockholm immediately for a series of meetings in the ornate Parliamentary building. There was a question that had been rattling around in my head ever since Betsy's telephone call.

'Is there any chance that Sweden could intervene and negotiate a deal between the Americans and the Soviets?' I asked Mr Nilsson and the assembled MPs.

This offered the Soviets a way out without losing face. It would also pressure the Americans. Beyond a point of irritation, it would show the US that they could no longer resolve the issue behind closed doors and demonstrate that their policy of intimidating the Siberians into leaving the Embassy had failed.

The response was overwhelming. A few days later, nine prominent MPs from all three major political parties in Sweden visited the Soviet Embassy in Stockholm to hand-deliver a confidential letter addressed to President Leonid Brezhnev. The letter carried the seal of the Swedish Parliament and contained one crucial detail: Sweden were offering asylum to the Siberian Seven.

It was the best news that we could have hoped for, but ironically we were forced to keep the story secret as the success of Sweden's offer depended on its confidentiality.

If the Campaign to free the Seven had a strategic turning point, this was the first bend in the road. Here was a third country involved in the issue with a serious initiative that could not be ignored, even if the offer was never taken up. We had succeeded in Sweden with something that we were still striving to accomplish in Britain. Undoubtedly, the story made waves in political circles.

Have a Heart, Mr Brezhnev!

Lida Vashchenko started a hunger strike during the closing days of December, 1981, to seek to resolve their case.
She was pushing the envelope but it was disturbing
news with potentially disastrous consequences.

The international media sensed the personal drama
would make gripping news and television crews and
journalists descended on our tiny one-room Campaign
office at *Buzz* magazine, in South Wimbledon. I told BBC
TV news, 'Lida is fasting as a personal appeal to God but
her hunger strike may be seen as a tactic to petition the
politicians. I'm alarmed because I know her dedication
and resolve.'

The media gave generous coverage to an appeal made
by Lady Coggan, 'Have a heart, Mr Brezhnev – let these
families go', but when I telephoned Lyuba in Moscow
she was despondent and dismissive.

'Well, that's good,' Lyuba replied solemnly, 'but if you
really want to help us then go to the summit between Haig
and Gromyko and appeal to them. They're meeting in four
days' time in Geneva. Maybe they can resolve our situation.'

Her response left me depressed and exhausted. I had
spent every single day of the last seven months working
on their Campaign and a great effort had gone into organ-
ising Lady Coggan's press conference, which had been
deemed a success. What hope could we have of reaching
the US and Soviet foreign ministers in the next few days?

Supporters called from around the country to say that
radio stations were plugging Lady Coggan's appeal but
when they asked what could be done, all I could mutter
in frustration was, 'Pray, just pray. There's nothing anyone can do.'

The telephone rang again. The caller, with a strong
Scottish accent, introduced himself as George Robertson,

a Labour Party MP. He said, 'Some time ago, you wrote to our leader, Michael Foot. We've just been talking and he's asked me to assure you of the Labour Party's support for your Campaign. Is there anything we can do?'

'The only thing you can do is take up the case with Haig and Gromyko when they meet in Geneva,' I said dismissively, repeating what I had heard Lyuba say to me just thirty minutes earlier. I was abrasive, bordering on rudeness, my frustration seeping through every word I heard myself speak. Somehow George stayed on the line.

The idea was impossible but I tossed it out. To my surprise, he quizzed me further and agreed that the summit was a good opportunity to gain international exposure for the case.

Suddenly, the exhaustion left my body and I could feel a rush of adrenaline hit me. I sat bolt upright, my mind racing. The man on the telephone that I was insulting was the Labour Party's Foreign Affairs Spokesman. He didn't share my pessimism; in fact, he talked as though this impossible idea was achievable.

Without thinking, I heard myself say, 'George, is there any possibility that you could go to Geneva for us?'

'Well, I've got several meetings coming up but I don't think there's anything I couldn't switch,' George replied. 'Of course, I'll need to be briefed. Could we meet in the next hour?'

George Robertson was impressive in action. Within a short time he had grasped the substance of the story and was talking confidently with the news media in Geneva.

The international press needed a new angle and the Seven provided them with an ideal hook. One of Haig's top aides recognised George from a previous meeting in Washington and appointments were made for a fuller discussion later that evening. George also cornered the Soviet delegation and handed them a letter signed by several British politicians. Every opportunity that presented itself was seized. It was a *tour de force* performance by George.

The superpowers were given a resounding message in Geneva. Britain had forced the case of the Siberian Seven on to the agenda.

I knew that Haig and Gromyko weren't going to interrupt their summit to order the release of the Siberians, but we had succeeded in a strategic objective: the Siberian Seven could no longer be ignored. The process that had started in Sweden had taken a giant leap forward in Geneva.

We had reached the turning point in the case.

* * * *

Saturday, 30 January 1982 turned out to be our longest day. The top news story on all the BBC TV bulletins filled us with alarm.

LIDA VASHCHENKO, ONE OF THE SIBERIAN SEVEN, IS LEAVING THE AMERICAN EMBASSY IN MOSCOW, TO BE HOSPITALISED AFTER FEARS FOR HER HEALTH.

Everyone with a television set watched Lida walk by herself to an Embassy vehicle for the short drive to Moscow's Botkin Hospital. She appeared fragile but serene after a thirty-two day hunger strike.

The Siberian Seven had beaten the Falklands War to the top slot and the media deluged our office in Wimbledon. Would she be arrested? Would she disappear?

The news was chilling. One reporter suggested that Lida had a death wish. It might be good news, he speculated, such a sacrifice would force the hand of the superpowers.

I was restless. But what could we do?

While talking with Keston College's super sleuth, Mike Rowe, an idea evolved. That evening I did a circuit of media interviews starting with the BBC, confident that some Soviet snoop would pick up the broadcast. I had an important story to break.

Our Campaign purchased an airline ticket from Moscow to London on the same day she left the Embassy and Moscow's SAS office, in Kuznetsku Most 3, confirmed that Ticket No 1174403708294 named Lida Vashchenko as the passenger.

The ticket cost £395 and was purchased at a time when our finances were dangerously low and we needed every penny. The money spent at such a precarious time was proof that we really believed that she would be free. It was the physical evidence of our faith.

The last interview was with Dave Loyn at LBC, London's only talk radio station. As I talked about the ticket, Dave looked at me as though I was crazy. But he couldn't argue with the facts. We had a real airline ticket. The passenger's name was Lida Vashchenko. And Dave Loyn was holding the ticket in his hand.

*   *   *   *

The ticket was never used: after recovering, Lida went back to Siberia to look after her younger brothers and sisters.

The Campaign had made a mark and even the Kremlin were using traditional propaganda channels such as Tass and Radio Moscow to communicate their policy, but backstage tensions, misunderstandings, problems and lack of funds threatened. When the bank froze our account, Joan Edgar, now our only full-time worker, helped me pack our materials into cardboard boxes and we moved everything from *Buzz* magazine's Wimbledon office into my home in Abbey Wood. The Campaign files sat next to my Elvis vinyl.

To me things were clear. We had to remain resolute in campaigning and try to hold the organisation together. It wasn't an easy time.

Margaret Thatcher's second personal letter gave us a boost. Written at the time of the Falkands War, it was evidence that our Campaign had achieved another key objective. The Prime Minister declared that Britain would offer asylum to the Siberian Seven; essentially repeating the offer Sweden had made over a year ago.

We immediately cranked out copies of the Prime Minister's message to our supporters. The letter was a kind of trophy and I wanted everyone to share in its triumph.

But not everyone welcomed her message with appropriate reverence. When the letter was left on the photocopier, my cat, Durango Rolling Thunder, left muddy footprints across the page as he scrambled across the living room one wet afternoon.

All the major moves had been played. We had done everything we could. Now we had to maintain the pressure. Who could predict just what would happen next?

The future was like a castle under siege.

7

Release 1983

I always believed it would happen but when it happened I couldn't believe it.

The US Consul was on the telephone from Moscow. 'Lida's going to be released! She's coming out tomorrow.' It was electrifying news, and even the American official sounded shaken. 'Can you meet her in Austria and co-ordinate her arrival?'

In Vienna, Felix Block, the acting American Ambassador, was jovial and acted more like an accomplice than a diplomat. He told me that there had been unprecedented interest in the Siberians and that a decision had been taken at the highest political level to 'clear it up'. He walked over to his desk and clutched a bundle of cables. 'Just look what came in overnight,' he said. 'They're going crazy in Washington.'

We set off for the airport in the Embassy's limousine but parted before we reached the terminal building. 'Tell me what you want and we'll arrange it,' he said conspiratorially. 'But we can't be directly involved.'

Lida arrived on a smoky April evening. Despite the secrecy, the story had leaked out to the international media and a pack of reporters stalked the exits of Vienna's crowded terminal searching for signs of their prey.

Mysteriously, airport security located me in the busy terminal building and I was ushered into a small, airless room.

And there she was, Lida Vashchenko, frail, fragile, even tinier than I had recalled, fired with an inner strength, the first step in the fulfilment of her family's twenty-two year old dream. Last minute details were hastily arranged and we started the short walk to the exit. The getaway vehicle, a black Porsche, was parked at a side entrance of the airport to dispatch us to a nearby hotel. As we stepped out of the airport's security area, the media swooped. Television cameras, flash bulbs blazing, reporters firing questions. Everyone was desperate to hear the first words from the girl who had forced the superpowers to release her from captivity.

For the first time, we tried to dodge the press. It was agreed that Lida would be careful with her words. The Soviets were watching, her family waiting. Back in the USSR.

The media camped outside our hotel as the pressure for interviews intensified. Mike Rowe and Dirk Jan Groot, from the Dutch Campaign group, jetted in to help.

Political manoeuvres and intrigue intensified. Even White House representatives flew in to meet with us. Lida's mood swings matched her decisions, changing by the hour. One American official became fairly agitated. 'She's got to go to Israel. Get her on the first flight. That's all,' he told me.

I was determined that Lida should make her own decisions but she said she would pray about the decision and agreed within an hour.

The Americans were delighted but relentless. They forced the Israelis to open their Embassy minutes after Sabbath ended to process our visas and within hours,

Lida, myself and Ray Barnett, another activist, were on Israeli soil.

The next few weeks in Israel were equally turbulent as almost every new day brought another twist. News from Siberia influenced Lida's moods and when some telephone calls weren't connected, she was convinced that the Soviets had a sinister motive, plunging her into a deeper depression.

My objective was to keep Lida away from the press but somehow I found myself (with Ray Barnett) at a meeting with a big American Christian media agency. The executive had been assigned the task of securing an interview for her boss, a high profile Christian leader.

'I don't think that's such a good idea,' I said and explained why we wanted Lida to remain low key.

'Look, our leader is flying in tomorrow and he's only doing two interviews. One is with the President of Israel and the other is with Lida,' she snapped.

The television executive was clearly under pressure from her bosses in the US to place their No 1 with this top news story. Under different circumstances, we would have grabbed the exposure but I knew the Soviets would be watching every move Lida made and I didn't want to jeopardise them granting exit visas for her family.

The woman persisted but when it was clear that I wasn't going to change my mind, she erupted in fury. 'Doesn't Lida realise that we bought her?' she yelled at me, slamming her glass down on the table, startling the people nearby.

'No one bought her. No one owns her,' I replied. I knew if I didn't leave immediately I would be unable to control my temper. I paid for my Coke and left Ray to pick up the pieces.

In fact, I had another meeting with yet another Christian group who wanted to use Lida to promote some new scheme. The previous meeting forced me to make a decision. It was seductive living on room service in hotels, mixing with the 'movers and shakers', and 'helping Lida'. But was this what I wanted to do with my life? I walked along Tel Aviv's stony beach and within half an hour I knew what I had to do.

Lida had to determine for herself how she used her freedom. She was comfortable with Ray Barnett and I handed in my notice as a 'minder'. Beyond that, the Siberians had recently left the American Embassy in Moscow and were back home in Chernogorsk. I had a Campaign to run.

Lida didn't object and within twenty-four hours I was booked on an early morning flight back to London.

Back in Abbey Wood, Joan had kept the office running and Piccadilly Radio's Bryce Cooke travelled down from Cheadle Hume to help with communication. The Campaign continued as though nothing had happened but Lida's release had fired us with the hope that it would soon be over. For three years we had campaigned. Knocked on every imaginable door. Pleaded for support from anyone who could help. Urged Christians everywhere to pray. The wall remained steel cold, iron hard.

*   *   *   *

With theatrical precision, the Soviets released the Vashchenko family on 27 June 1983, five years to the exact day that their ordeal in the Embassy had begun. Fifty-five days after Lida's release, we assembled in Vienna for an extraordinary reunion.

The media frenzy intensified as tempers flared but the correspondents from *Time* magazine and *Newsweek* took charge. Everyone got their story and the Siberian Seven made the front page of newspapers around the world.

One month later, the scene was re-enacted, one last time. Twenty-one year old Timothy, his new bride, Tatyana, and thirteen members of the Chmykhalov family touched down briefly in Vienna, en route to America. Again, tears of relief, of joy, and abundant thanks to God.

In Vienna, I showed Timothy our latest newsletter with the headline: Pray that 1983 will be the year of his release. He held the leaflet in his hand for a few minutes repeating the words aloud, and then said, emotionally, 'It came true.'

But why were they freed? Whatever top level deal had been fixed between the superpowers, without the dynamic combination of prayer, campaigning, political pressure and publicity, it's likely that these two Christian families would have remained at the bottom of the 'Fix It' list.

One hundred days marked the miracles of release. Every time I skipped a heartbeat.

Truly, trusting God can take you to the limit, the edge. But sometimes, it's at the barricades when life seems beyond hope, out of reach of man's solutions, that you stray across the borderline of faith and trusting God becomes your highest calling.

I caught a glimpse of that faith as Moscow caught me adrift, holidaying from my commitments. The Campaign and encounters in Moscow had changed the direction of my life.

The Players

The Siberian Seven Campaign was the first Christian-led initiative to capture such major news coverage and the first to use the national media and the political system to communicate a message and to seek to influence events by doing so. It was to set the model for other projects that followed on a variety of issues. The Campaign lasted three years and many of the characters had stories to tell…

- The Vashchenko family stayed briefly in Israel and then settled in towns across the west coast of America.
- The Chmykhalovs lived in Dallas for several years and then moved west to California where they now live.
- Peter Meadows went on to numerous exploits, including the setting up of Premier Radio. *Buzz* magazine, the publication that Peter started as a photocopied sheet at home, survived several reincarnations and is presently *Christianity+Renewal*.
- Dan Wooding first urged that we start a campaign and recommend that Peter should hire me to run it. He moved from the *Sunday People* in Fleet Street to Orange County, in California where he runs Assist News Service, and is the author of some forty-one books.
- David Alton was the first MP that Bill Hampson, an activist, contacted and his commitment to us never wavered. After eighteen years as Member of Parliament for Liverpool (Penny Lane and Strawberry Fields were in his constituency, he reminded me recently) he was honoured as Lord Alton of Liverpool and continues to use his influence to help the oppressed.
- George Robertson moved to the House of Lords and headed up the Nato Alliance. A few years ago, George was accused of being a Soviet spy and sued the source of the accusation. I was pleased to provide a statement documenting George's support for the Siberian Seven for the libel case.

- Felix Block, the friendly diplomat in Austria, hit the headlines in the US. He was accused of passing secrets to the Soviets amid other accusations of spying.
- The first person to support the Siberian Seven was the nuclear scientist Dr Andrei Sakharov. He was visiting the consular section of the American Embassy and noticed the Seven, standing in the corner, during their first few days in the building in 1978. He promised to help and wrote two letters to Brezhnev, urging him to grant them exit visas. Sakharov told the Siberians, 'Don't expect too much. Brezhnev never replies to my letters.'
- Joan Baez was the first celebrity to add her name to a letter that we were co-ordinating to *The Times* of London. Friends at Humanitas, her human rights group, donated a generous amount to us following one of her London concerts.
- John Cleese, Vladimir Bukovsky, Malcolm Muggeridge, Count Nikolai Tolstoy, Tom Stoppard, James Fox, Judi Dench and Glenda Jackson were among many who sent messages. When we asked Cliff Richard to sign a petition, he replied, 'Their plight certainly underlies how easy we Christians have it this side of the curtain. The signing of my name seems a pathetic move when one considers the suffering involved, but if it helps, here it is.'
- The chess grandmaster, Victor Korchnoi, pulled out of a meeting at the last moment. His excuse was simply that his family were finally arriving in Israel after receiving those precious exit visas from the Soviets. We were disappointed, but delighted for him. His telegram read, 'Thanks for understanding the situation. Next time you can count on me.'
- The Siberians were Pentecostal believers but the Pentecostal churches in the west reacted cautiously.

However, within their own circles, the case made waves. Eventually, one of their prominent leaders, Eric Dando, decided something must be done and his intervention influenced his own denomination to support the Campaign.

8

Jailhouse Rock 1984

The Campaign to Free the Siberian Seven had been successful – the Seven and their families were free. I was out of a job.

The Campaign had its way of extending its circle. I, for one, joined for three and a half days a week, strictly for two months. Joan Edgar joined for six weeks, to help organise Human Wrongs Day. Joan was someone who would do the right thing, even when no one was watching. She had become a faithful worker and a best friend. When the Campaign started three years earlier, no one could have predicted that it would have ended for Joan and I, on 7 January 1984, with Timothy Chmykhalov being the best man at our wedding.

All my money had been spent on the Campaign. I had no savings in the bank to pay the mortgage. My job prospects were dismal. My career was non-existent. Joan must have been full of faith. She was also in love.

Peter Meadows' wedding gift was a holiday that became our honeymoon. An unexpected personal collection for us, taken at a meeting arranged by Gerald Coates from the Cobham Fellowship, covered our wedding expenses. It was a relief not to start married life with a debt. My friend, Dirk Jan Groot in Holland, cajoled a Dutch television company into appointing me as their London correspondent and a few days' work paid our expenses for the month. Later, when we moved to Cobham, Gerald contributed to our support through Pioneer, but with little finances coming in and with a young family, the pressures intensified for Joan.

In Moscow, everything that I believed had been put to the test. The question that I carried with me was simply this: what did I want to do with my life?

The question answered itself with news from Leningrad in 1983. Valeri Barinov had been arrested.

*   *   *   *

In 1981, while planning a visit to the Siberian Seven, a friend from the Ichthus Fellowship in South London asked if I would play postman and carry a gift for someone in Leningrad.

With Joan and Timothy Chmykhalov outside Down Street. Our next appointment was at the Dietrich Bonhoeffer Church in South London, where Timothy served as the best man at our wedding.

Photo: Mick Rock

Sure, I said, and promptly forgot about it.

When it arrived, I was shocked to see a bright red guitar. How will I get this through customs without creating suspicion, I inquired. The reply came, 'We'll pray for you.'

Russian customs officials had a simple rule. Everyone was prey. At Moscow's airport, our queue moved the slowest. As we inched nearer the front, I realised the official checking our line was going through everyone's luggage with military precision. On the counter beside him were contraband that had been seized. Books. Tapes. Clothes. A friend had told me that he had witnessed an incident when one customs officer held up a book to his colleague and said in Russian, 'Do you want to read this?' When the official nodded, the book was seized. There was no appeal.

I was sure that the guitar would be confiscated. With just one passenger in front of me, all my carefully rehearsed series of answers sounded ludicrous. My anxiety level was high and rising.

I was concentrating so intensely that I hadn't noticed that a new counter had opened up alongside us to reduce the lengthy queue and the customs official assigned to the post was pointing directly at me.

I stumbled my way across to the new line. I could hear several other passengers move swiftly behind me.

The moment had come. I held up my battered suitcase and the guitar case. The customs official was a young man and he smiled when he saw the guitar. 'Beatles? You like Beatles?'

'Yes,' I answered nervously. 'I like the Beatles.'

'Beatles are good. I like Beatles,' he said enthusiastically.

He proceeded to name his favourite Beatles songs. I quickly agreed that the same songs were also my favourites.

He raised his eyebrows when I told him I was visiting Russia on holiday. 'I want go Liverpool for holiday,' he said wistfully. 'Beatles,' he contributed, as explanation. We both nodded.

After a few perfunctory questions, he handed me back my passport, we shook hands and I was waved through. I walked quickly through the customs hall and never looked back.

The guitar was in.

The gift was for Valeri Barinov, Leningrad's notorious rock preacher.

Travelling beyond Leningrad's city limits, Valeri's world stirred me deeply. He moved with a quality of grace and a recklessness of faith. Once more, I was confronted with someone who was paying a high price for something that I had taken lightly.

Weeks after my visit, Valeri sent me a message asking for a synthesiser; at the same time, we were given a generous gift and I felt compelled to use the money for Valeri's request. This time I called my friends in Ichthus and asked them to carry the musical instrument and, again, it slipped past vigilant customs officers.

With miraculous timing, it arrived within days of Valeri's recording schedule. Valeri and his group had planned secret recordings of *Trumpet Call*, a rock musical about the second coming of Christ. The project was the fulfilment of an eight year old dream and the recording had been meticulously planned for months. Just hours later and the synthesiser wouldn't have been used on the recording.

The BBC World Service broadcast *Trumpet Call* in Russian and it caused a sensation, turning Valeri into a local hero. Soviet censors jammed further broadcasts. Sometime later, when the BBC technicians went on strike, pre-recorded music replaced the regular schedules and the censors relaxed their vigilance. Perhaps the Russian guardians of the minds had gone out for a smoke, as no one seemed to notice that the music filling the uncensored airwaves was Valeri's trumpet call to the world.

But Valeri's music was proving too dangerous and, when he was arrested, we recognised the fingerprints of the KGB.

News from inside Valeri's labour camp was sparse but alarming, and following reports that he had suffered a heart attack, we intensified our campaign. David Alton visited his family with practical help. Tapes of *Trumpet Call* were smuggled out of Russia and with support from Ichthus, Keston College, Word Records and others, we released the secret recordings.

We thought publicity and pressure were our best weapons and secured wide coverage including the *Sun*, *The Times* and *New Musical Express*; David Alton enlisted the support of both Neil Kinnock and David Steel, the leaders of the Labour and Liberal Parties. When I was interviewed by ITV news, Valeri's music was broadcast on television for the first time.

I was on a freelance assignment for Dutch television when we heard that Neil Kinnock was visiting Moscow. I drafted the text of a telegram requesting his help and left it with Joan to phone through to the post office. Around midday she called me and said, 'The telegram to Mr Kinnock will cost £30.' Knowing that our finances were at breaking point, we discussed the impact it could make and decided we had no option.

That Sunday a friend called and said that they were praying for Valeri. They hoped Mr Kinnock's intervention would help.

'What are you talking about?' I asked incredulously.

'I saw the story in the *Sunday Times*,' my friend replied.

'But I bought the *Sunday Times* and didn't see the story,' I said, somewhat agitated. People were always saying they'd seen a story in one paper but in fact it turned out to be somewhere else. 'Which page is it on?' I demanded.

'The front page,' came the terse retort.

And there it was. On the front page. Mr Kinnock was on the case. I had skimmed the paper but missed the story; under a feature about Russia, a bullet point covered Kinnock's visit and our campaign.

Sometime later we learned the background to the story. When Joan was sending our telegram, we had failed to learn the name of Mr Kinnock's hotel; in frustration, she had directed it to the British Embassy with a prayer that it would be passed on. In fact, Mr Kinnock had been staying at the British Embassy and it had been placed in his hands while he was being interviewed by reporters from the *Sunday Times*.

It was the last time we would hesitate about spending our pennies on campaigning…

*　*　*　*

Valeri Barinov was raised in a state orphanage and joined the army as a teenager. In his own words, he was a rebel. 'I was a bad man. A punk. I would be drunk all the time, fight with people.'

Contemplating suicide, the ringing of a cathedral bell caused him to pull back, and he eventually came to faith. Evangelism was outlawed in the Soviet Union, but Valeri spoke fearlessly and was well known amongst Leningrad's street people, drunks and prostitutes. In communist youth clubs, he would deliver his version of popular rock songs and preach about Jesus in between numbers. He should have been awarded a gold record for endeavour. Instead the Russians rewarded him with a criminal record.

In October 1983, Valeri was arrested and held in a psychiatric hospital. His wife, Tanya, was told, 'Your husband's views on religion differ so much from those of ordinary citizens that he needs psychiatric treatment.' Arrested for trying to 'escape', in 1984, he was held in the KGB headquarters in Leningrad as a high-risk prisoner. At his trial Valeri declared to the court, 'My crime is I'm a Christian.' He continued his pilgrimage of faith through the midnight world of the Gulag prison network and the psychiatric terror of Soviet prison hospitals.

Mike Morris, of the Evangelical Alliance, was a close friend and worked in tight partnership with us. He

David Alton's visit to Tanya Barinova. Left to right: Bill Hampson, Tanya Barinova, David Alton and David Campanale. Both Bill and David Campanale were active supporters.

visited Valeri just days after his release in 1986 and learned the extent of the rock preacher's illness and the impact of his faith. Mike observed that Valeri's eyes were alive but his body was weak from illness, a heart attack and beatings received in the labour camp. His home for the last two years had been a labour camp, chillingly named 'Blood Camp'.

Suffering and death there were everyday occurrences and the administration frequently instructed informants to kill a troublesome prisoner. The authorities saw their chance to get rid of Valeri when he fell ill with pleurisy. 'I was very sick and unable to do anything. The camp bosses didn't want me to recover and told the local medical staff not to treat me.'

With water dripping from the walls and ceiling of the cell where inmates slept on the floor, there was little hope of warmth and things seemed bleak. As the strength ebbed away from his body and the cold moved into it, he prayed, asking God to let him die. God answered through the very men who had once kicked Valeri senseless. During the freezing nights, fellow prisoners kept him warm by huddling around him on the floor. It was further proof that God had touched the lives of the prisoners at Blood Camp.

'My faith in Jesus was all that sustained me in Blood Camp. I would not be alive if God had not loved and protected me. I knew that if I was in prison and tortured it was so that I could tell other prisoners about Jesus.'

But his trail through the archipelago of Gulag was marked by those prisoners – now witnesses – who found faith through his testimony. Incredibly, some were even baptised in their prison cells.

'God gave me supernatural strength to endure this torment. I spent several weeks and months in punishment cells for telling people about Jesus. When the jailers came to me, I would say, "God bless you." They were amazed that I did not hate them but tried to love them. Even in the punishment cell, I was able to tell prisoners about Jesus and some believed.'

Mike returned from Leningrad with news of Valeri's appeal to Mikhail Gorbachev: 'Let me preach the gospel in Russia or let me go.'

We were able to pass Valeri's appeal to Mrs Thatcher before her official visit to the Soviet Union in 1987 and days after she left the country, local emigration officials telephoned Valeri and told him he would be allowed to leave if he completed some formalities. When the invitation I sent Valeri and his family, formalised through solicitors and the Foreign Office, arrived in Leningrad, the officials told him to pack his bags and leave within two days. But with typical panache, Valeri insisted that he – not the authorities – would set his date for departure.

The Barinov family's triumphant arrival at Heathrow. This photo says it all.   Photo Chris Gander

He spent his last few weeks in Russia travelling to various cities and sharing his faith. In October, he gathered a group outside a Leningrad cathedral. Once an ornate church, it had been turned into an atheist museum. Several hundred people gathered for this open-air mission and the inevitable happened; Valeri was arrested and held for several hours in the local police station.

When I reached him on the telephone, I expressed sympathy to hear that they were fined fifty roubles, knowing their meagre resources. But Valeri laughed, 'The fine was OK. If we hired a hall for a meeting, with a sound system, and everything else, it would have cost us over three hundred roubles. This was only fifty roubles. It was cheap.'

Valeri's arrival was a magical moment, captured on BBC TV *News*. Media coverage was high over the next few weeks. *Christian Family* magazine launched an appeal to raise money to buy Valeri a house on the coast where he settled.

Driving through the streets of London one night, shortly after his arrival, we cruised down London's Regent Street. It was past midnight and the brightly coloured decorative neon advertised a secularised Christmas. But Valeri was enthralled and turned to me, somewhat wistfully, and said, 'I can't believe this is happening. It's like a gift to us.' My instinctive observation was that Valeri was a gift to the church in the west.

9

Proclaiming Jubilee

David Alton played a singularly significant role and his commitment to us never faltered for a second. Without him alongside us, I don't know how far we would have got. He launched Jubilee Campaign in Parliament's aptly titled Jubilee Room, in February 1987, with the deceptively simple idea of asking other MPs to 'adopt' prisoners of faith around the world.

Working with a team drawn primarily from the Cobham Fellowship, Rosie McLaughlin squeezed extra hours out of the day to mobilise her army of volunteers to prepare 'prisoner case files' and to select a sumptuous array of international delicacies. Parliamentary rules prohibited food being taken into the rooms but we found a creative way through the bureaucratic maze. We decided not to request permission. If we didn't ask, they couldn't refuse.

The response was impressive, as MPs appreciated our inventiveness. Word quickly spread that you could sample a rare Ukrainian beer, an unusual selection of fresh fruit and ethnic nibbles in the Jubilee Room. More importantly, about thirty MPs 'adopted' prisoners of faith on the spot.

David Alton 'adopted' Valeri Barinov and his case secured a victory with his arrival in Britain in November 1987. The diplomatic salvos fired from within Parliament over the next few months hit targets all across the world, as MPs took action for cases they had 'adopted'. They were also making the news, both nationally and locally, as the media reported the intense lobbying.

Sometimes the timing was extraordinary…

After meeting Timothy Renton, the Foreign Office minister, about a Romanian prisoner, I was having coffee with David Alton and mentioned that I'd heard that the Turkish Government had imposed a ban on the Bible. Later that evening, David's researcher, David Campanale, telephoned. 'David Steel has an official meeting with Turgut Ozal, Turkey's Prime Minister, shortly. How quickly can you get us a report documenting the ban?'

We raced a report out. Raced to the House of Commons with it. David raced to Mr Steel's office with it to find Mr Steel racing for his meeting with the Turkish Prime Minister. It was breathless but exhilarating.

After completing his official business, Mr Steel raised the issue of censorship with Mr Ozal. Somewhat baffled, the Turkish Prime Minister disputed such an allegation, whereupon Mr Steel produced our report, hot off the typewriter. The censorship of the Bible. The freedom of the press. Etc. Clearly some misunderstanding, Mr Ozal intimated, but I'll look into it. Keep me informed, Mr Steel smiled.

The initiative required no further action, just a prayerful watch. Some months later, the Turkish Ministry of the Interior published an official decree formally lift- ing the ban on the Bible.

* * * *

If I Can't Help, Who Can?

Friends from the Ichthus Fellowship asked us to take up the case of a young man imprisoned in Nicosia, Cyprus. Erdinc Ucjac, a Kurd of Turkish origin, had been arrested with two young people from Youth With a Mission, but when both were released, he was held without charge for several months. When the prosecutor eventually pressed charges, Erdinc's defence lawyers weren't permitted to see any details. We documented this flagrant abuse of the law and sent the case, among others, to Cyril Townsend, MP, one of the MPs who wanted to join our adoption programme.

Mr Townsend telephoned us the following day. 'I can't believe this. Surely there must be a stronger case against him than the details you have sent me?' he said, genuinely baffled.

Richard Warnes, our Parliamentary Officer, assured Mr Townsend that our sources were reliable and after some further verification on specific points, Mr Townsend was reassured. He said, 'I am hopeful that I can do something. I am currently Chairman of the British-Cyprus Commonwealth Parliamentary Association. If I can't help, then who can?'

As a direct result of Mr Townsend's intervention, Erdinc was released from prison and allowed to leave Cyprus to live in freedom. Richard was a former army officer, a physical exercise fanatic, with an impressive and colourful vocabulary, but the power of this encounter left him speechless. Out of 651 MPs in Parliament, we had been directed to the only one who could really make a difference.

Death Row, South Africa

When the Sharpeville Six were sentenced to death in South Africa, both Mike Morris and I felt compelled to make a gesture to demonstrate that we would not remain silent and passive while such a tragedy unfolded. We had just a few days to muster a response.

Flimsy evidence convicted them of being accomplices in the murder of the township's deputy mayor, who had been killed during the unrest that broke out following a rise in house rents and legislative changes that excluded the black population from local government. Although their subsequent trial never produced evidence to prove their involvement, they were sentenced to death based on their 'collective guilt'.

Mike co-ordinated a massive petition at Spring Harvest entitled simply 'Appeal for Mercy'. At the time

Protestors recruited by Mike Morris at Spring Harvest protest in London. Photo: The *Guardian*

we didn't know that Theresa Ramashamola, a Christian, had summarised her court statement with just those words. We assembled a prison cell, gallows and coffin, all on top of a lorry, with prison uniform for our recruits, many drawn from Spring Harvest.

We'd arranged to meet everyone at 11am at platform 1 at Waterloo Station and quickly stepped into our prison uniforms. Some of our 'convicts' started handing out literature about the Sharpeville Six, attracting the attention of several British Rail passengers.

Visually the exercise was arresting. It also attracted the attention of the police, who told me to clear the concourse immediately or I'd face arrest. Since we hadn't actually started our demonstration, we took the two minute warning and moved to the House of Commons where photographers and television cameras caught MPs as they jostled to take their turn in the prison cell. They also queued to sign our petition.

The next stop was the South African Embassy but at Trafalgar Square the police again threatened me with arrest for not securing authorised permission for such an event. After seeing the lorry, complete with prison cell, gallows and coffin, the police said that they would give us a few minutes to hand our petition in to the authorities and to say a prayer.

I didn't tell the police that our original plan was to drive the lorry on to the pavement outside the Embassy and deflate the tyres, thereby giving us extended residency of the pavement. Since the police had my name and address, I felt sure that they would not be amused.

Just as we were handing in our petition, I noticed our driver squatting by the rear tyre of the truck and caught Rosie's look of panic. Her eyes told me that she had forgotten to tell the driver that we'd changed our plans...

Thankfully, the worldwide outrage forced the South African government to commute the death sentences of the Sharpeville Six the day before their execution on 18 March 1988.

Jailed at the Top of the World

The reports from Nepal, the world's only Hindu kingdom, were devastating; churches attacked, Christians imprisoned and a father arrested for arranging a Christian burial for his child. There were many sensitivities, as missionary groups were concerned that 'campaigning' would affect their status. When the head of the Bible Society, on behalf of local church leaders, personally asked us for help, we launched a campaign to seek changes in the law.

My friend Charles Mendies, in Nepal, helped us document two decades of persecution from 1970 to 1988 and spoke at a special hearing in Parliament, organised by David Alton, when the report was launched. Charles pointed out that despite this intense persecution, the indigenous church remained strong. In 1960, there were virtually no baptised Christian believers in Nepal, but the number had grown to 25,000 people by 1990.

We knew Charles was taking a risk. He was in the UK while on bail, facing a prison sentence for 'preaching'. When Charles was featured in a magazine published by the Gideons, he was arrested, the editorial was used as evidence, and he was sentenced to one thousand days in jail.

With *Christian Family* magazine, we launched a campaign for Charles but I was disturbed that his involvement with us might have contributed to his imprisonment. I flew immediately to Nepal to offer practical help to his family and to try to meet Charles, if possible.

Kathmandu is a dazzling, exotic city set amid the awesome splendour of the spectacular Himalayan mountain range. Samantha Fox posters and Rambo IV videos in the bazaar were visual reminders that tourism and western values had made inroads into this once hidden, mysterious land. During the sixties, Kathmandu became a mystical haven on the hippie trail. It was the focal point of pilgrimage for the lost youth of western civilisation who trekked up the mountain in search of the answers to the mysteries of life.

Susan, Charles's wife, combined resilience and determination, with a clear sense of responsibility and realism. She told me, 'I was shocked when the police arrested Charles. We could have left the country, escaped, but why should we? We are Nepali and proud of our land, our home. If this is the price we must pay for being true to the Christian faith, then so be it. Charles and I knew it would be hard but we are prepared to be apart for the next three years.'

The day after I arrived in the hilltop kingdom, Susan took me to Central Jail, about fifteen minutes away. Prisoners met their families at one of the jail's gates, under the close supervision of armed guards. Behind cold steel bars, the prisoners peered through padlocked gates. Five feet away, we huddled together in the street with everyone else, straining for a better view.

Seven prisoners stood shoulder to shoulder inside the jail, each one shouting messages to the outside world. Mothers and wives, fathers and sons, shouted back their replies, sometimes simultaneously.

The jail held seven hundred prisoners and Charles shared a cell with seventeen others. Victor, a Russian, was on a murder charge. Michael, from Reading, was caught dealing drugs.

When his young son, Daniel, saw his father, he rushed forward. 'Daddy!' It was a poignant scene as father and son covered the five foot distance with their eyes and embraced with a smile.

Charles said he realised the risks. 'I could be in prison for three years,' he said, through the bars of the prison. 'It's in God's hands. I'm ready to serve him wherever I am.'

Susan signalled that we should leave. Charles called out to Daniel who sat perched in my arms, listening intently to our conversation. 'Come, my son, come to Dad.'

Without thinking, Daniel stepped down and moved towards the bars of the jail where Charles crouched down with outstretched hands.

But the guard stepped in. 'No!' he said firmly. No physical contact was permitted and nothing could be slipped to the prisoners.

Little Daniel extended his arm and for a precarious moment the orders were disobeyed as their fingers touched for a second. The crowd appeared to have hushed, intently observing this human drama being enacted, for each one in Central Jail completely understood the significance of this embrace between father and son.

But it was not to be and Daniel stood in the dusty street, waving goodbye to Papa.

Through it all Susan remained steadfast, and back at the family home, she evoked a remarkable calmness amidst the turmoil she must have felt. 'I have experienced a sense of God's presence. I believe it is a privilege to suffer for the Lord.'

*   *   *   *

At the UN

Susan told me about recent attacks on churches and helped me slip into another jail to visit Pastor Tir Bahadur Dewan, aged seventy-eight, who started the first Nepali Church in the country.

Two van loads of police raided his church at Bhaktapur, and seized the entire congregation of thirty-nine people. Many were badly beaten and religious literature was confiscated as police ransacked the church. When we visited the area, even local people were dismayed at the way police manhandled the elderly preacher and some of the women.

David Armstrong from OM had recently set up a film business, Send The Vision. He travelled with me and filmed wherever appropriate. As a result, we were able to place the story with BBC Television, while *The Times* and other papers gave us prominent coverage.

With the story running high in the media, I called on the government and was told that the British Foreign Office Minister met twice a year with his Nepalese counterpart and that the issue had been placed high on the agenda. It was encouraging news and an indication of the impact campaigning can make.

But we had another target. Our campaign had circulated a petition addressed to the United Nations. While most human rights issues were taken up within this arena, the plight of Christians had rarely been raised here. It was our aspiration to change that but it wasn't clear where to start.

I was dashing out of our small office in Richmond, when I was reminded of a 5pm meeting with a young American law student. I suspected that this was another earnest but naïve person who had the answer to the world's problems and wanted to take my time discussing her impractical theories for the next few hours. Before I could foist the meeting on to someone else, our guest was ushered into our cramped office. I was trapped.

Ann Buwalda perched on the edge of a table, and said, 'I've just been studying the UN legal system and am looking for a case study to take up. Can you help or do you know someone who can?'

I didn't reply but reached to the side of my desk, clutched a bundle of petitions to the UN and shoved them over to her.

The timing was startling.

Over the next few weeks Ann co-ordinated an intensive timetable of lobbying activities for the UN's Human Rights Commission in Geneva, and the Australian preacher John Smith flew over to deliver the main address. The impact was considerable and Ann returned to Washington and drummed up support on Capitol Hill, opening up another portal for the campaign.

There were whoops and cheers when Charles Mendies came on the phone just hours after he was freed to ask us to thank everyone who prayed and worked for his release from prison. Although things are still tough for Christians, the severe persecution seems to have paused for the moment.

Escape from Iran

Ann Buwalda finished her law degree, opened an office for Jubilee Campaign in Washington, and established her own immigration law practice, Just Law International PC, in Virginia. Ann's loyalty and commitment was humbling. She was a straight arrow and undertook many adventures of faith.

Ann was at lunch when she got a call from Azam, an Iranian woman living in America. Azam's story began fourteen years before, in Teheran, when she fled a violent, abusive marriage after being beaten almost to death. Under Iranian law, she automatically lost custody of her young children when she left for the United States and safety.

Azam's many cards, letters and presents never reached her children, who were told, instead, that their mother no longer cared about them. Her husband's violent nature meant the boys were often badly treated and neglected.

Then one day, Azam's son, Soheil, accidentally found a card from his mother. Realising that she had not abandoned them, he dialled the phone number and within seconds, mother and child were locked in an emotional reunion. Soheil shared the secret with his younger brother, Saman.

As their home life deteriorated further, both boys begged their mother to help them escape. In desperation, Azam spent all her savings and hired an Iranian smuggler to get her sons out of Iran. A hazardous twenty-hour trek through the mountains led to Turkey but once across the border, the boys were bundled into packing boxes for a three-hour bus ride bound for Bulgaria. The 'safe house' they had been promised turned out to be a mountain hideout for drug dealers and a route for international smugglers.

Frightened and alone, the teenagers grew increasingly alarmed with each passing day. A chance meeting with a friendly priest in the market place in Sofia enabled the boys to get away from the smugglers and over the next few weeks they sought refuge with local Christians. After attending church, they found personal faith and were baptised.

When Bulgarian police picked up the boys on the street, without travel documents, it was obvious they had entered the country illegally. They were thrown into jail and held in solitary confinement to await deportation back to Iran.

Neither Soheil or Saman needed any reminder that the penalty in Iran for converting to Christianity was death. An Iranian official visited them in jail and confirmed their fears. 'We have heard of your conversion,' he said. 'We will "take care" of you when we get you back in our custody.'

As an American citizen, Azam was able to apply for a visa on behalf of her younger son, Saman, and rescued him. But Soheil, already eighteen, was no longer a minor, and would have to make the application himself – in person!

The tension was rising as confusing information delayed the case. With each hour that passed, the danger increased for Soheil. The deportation order to Iran was on the table.

When Ann, in Washington, heard this story from Azam, she said 'We have to move fast.' She identified the countries where Soheil could register his application for asylum. The nearest was Austria. But the Austrian immigration authorities refused the youth a tourist visa. Ann understood the implications of this and flew imme-di-ately to Vienna to represent Soheil at the refugee hearings that were held there.

It was Thursday evening.

Soheil needed the tourist visa by 5pm Friday or he faced expulsion to Iran. The authorities were sorry. Orders were orders.

The deadline was now twenty-four hours away.

Ann forcefully mounted her legal resistance, clutching at every legal straw that she could, and contacted every possible office that could help. She accompanied Soheil to the refugee interview at the US consulate in Vienna and had to overcome a deceiving interpreter who was falsifying the Iranian youth's story. If Ann had not challenged and exposed this deception, Soheil's case would have failed.

The deportation hung over Soheil like a death sentence. This was developing all the suspense of a Hitchcock thriller. All that was needed was a Hollywood hero to ride the rescue...

Back in California, Azam, Soheil's mother, learned that one of the parents at the school where she worked was Gale Anne Hurd, the producer of blockbusters such as *The Terminator*. Gale reached for the telephone and dialled Arnold Schwarzenegger's number, and eventually reached him on the set of his new movie. When he realised how serious things were, he immediately contacted the Austrian government.

In Vienna, news came through that Soheil's asylum case had been granted and travel documents would be issued. Ann looked at her watch. It was 4.45pm. Just fifteen minutes later and it would have been too late.

Schwarzenegger's telephone call had made the difference. He had turned into a real life action hero in the best role of his life.

Soheil arrived in Los Angeles soon after with his brother Saman to a tearful reunion with his mother and to spend their first Christmas together in fourteen years.

Dangerous Graffiti

David Alton's idea of MPs adopting Prisoners of Faith had been a remarkable success, with over one hundred and fifty MPs joining us to take up Prisoners of Faith cases from countries as politically different as South Africa, Burma, China, Egypt, Vietnam, Nepal, Sudan, Iran, Guatemala, the Soviet Union and Eastern Europe.

It would take a book to recount the achievements and another book to explain just how much my life had been enriched.

The atlas of religious persecution had a panoramic swoop and global context. Historians observe that more Christians have been hounded and killed in the twentieth century than in the rest of Christian history combined. Around the world, living the faith was a crime.

While publicity and pressure were effective in reaching the communist authorities, a different approach was required when dealing with Islamic states, and in many instances we were required to keep our work confidential for fear of hindering the initiative or harming the individual.

In recent years, Christians in Pakistan have been subjected to intimidation, harassment and persecution on an unprecedented level. Some Christians have died in mysterious circumstances, while Naimat Ahmed, a Christian teacher, was stabbed to death in broad daylight.

In 1993, Fazul-ul-Haq, a Muslim priest in Pakistan, filed a complaint of blasphemy against eleven-year-old Salamat Masih, and two other Christians, Rehmat Masih and Manzoor Masih. The slim, elderly priest with a flowing white beard claimed that the trio had scribbled blasphemous words on the wall of his mosque in Gujrunwala, a large industrial city. Islamic Sharia law ruled that all three could be convicted on the word of a single witness. The penalty was death by hanging.

It was an unusual incident with sinister overtones. The boy was illiterate and only learned to write his name in prison. Personal disputes and tensions between Muslims and Christians appeared to be the motive for the complaint. The three Christians were charged under section 295-C of the Pakistan Penal Code but would a court really order a child to be executed? The Foreign Office was unaware of the incident when we contacted them but instructed its Embassy to take up the case and maintained pressure from that moment on. In the US, Ann mobilised support on Capitol Hill and an appeal was signed by American politicians Frank Wolf, Tom Lantos, Tony Hall and Christopher Smith.

Our friends at the *Sunday Express* were the first to report the story, in December 1993, and for once the text-book-style tabloid-newspaper headline seemed appropriate: GRAFFITI BOY FACES HANGMAN. One year later, we raised Salamat's case by name at the United Nations but the turning point came in April 1994.

After returning from a court appearance, the three defendants, Salamat, Rehmat and Manzoor, were with a group standing at a bus stop outside the court buildings on a bustling street in Lahore. The sudden violence took everyone by surprise. Hit men on motorbikes and the sound of gunfire in this drive-by shooting sent everyone running for cover.

Manzoor Masih took the full force of the assassin's guns. He died instantly, his body riddled with twelve bullets. Tragically, he left a widow with ten children. Rehmat was seriously wounded, and a church leader with them was shot in the face. Salamat was hit in the hand.

Their defence lawyer, Asma Jehangir, Pakistan's best known human rights advocate, had taken up the case after local lawyers had dropped their defence under pressure from fundamentalists. She told me, 'I was in a shop nearby when my office rang me on my mobile phone and told me that there had been a shooting.'

Asma rushed to the local hospital and as she was talking to one of the victims, he scribbled on a piece of paper and surreptitiously passed it to her. The note read: 'The man in blue behind you is the murderer.' Asma gasped and turned in astonishment. Her shocked reaction prompted the assassin to turn and flee.

The shooting sent shock waves around the world. Police investigating the murder of Manzoor Masih arrested the priest who had filed the original charge of blasphemy and three months after the shooting, the fury of the fundamentalists erupted in a weekend of frenzy.

At a Saturday afternoon public rally, in July 1994, Islamic leader, Maulana Darkhwasti, created a sensation by offering a one million rupee reward (about £20,000) to anyone who assassinated Pakistan's Minister of Law, Mr Syed Iqbal Haider, called 'the Salman Rushdie of Pakistan'. He had enraged the fundamentalists after an interview he had given in London to the BBC World Service had been broadcast in Pakistan.

Asma Jehangir – Pakistan's leading advocate on human rights issues.

The day before the interview, Mr Haider told David Alton and our Parliamentary Officer, Wilfred Wong, (who had raised the case of Salamat Masih and others) that amendments to the blasphemy law were being considered.

On the day of the rally, stickers appeared on buses and buildings throughout Lahore calling for the death of Asma Jehangir. The two coloured stickers had been distributed with that morning's edition of the English language newspaper, *The Dawn*, although how they were included with the paper remained a mystery.

Mrs Jehangir told me, 'The stickers say that I am the worst of all blasphemers. It is the duty of all Muslims to "find her and kill her."'

Encouraged by her friends, Asma Jehangir appointed a bodyguard armed with a Kalashnikov rifle, who followed her everywhere, including the courtroom, as she conducted Salamat's defence.

The extremists even targeted Prime Minister Benazir Bhutto, named in a blasphemy case in Pakistan's High Court, over statements she had once made about repealing the law.

On the day that Salamat's trial opened, in February 1995, a gunman was arrested on the roof of an adjacent building with a clear view into the courtroom. The man was later released by police.

That same month, the Judge finally delivered the verdict that everyone feared: death by hanging.

One week later, on 16 February, a violent demonstration at Lahore's High Court halted the application for bail and appeal that was being lodged. Outside the courtroom, a mob of about five hundred extremists insisted – loudly – that Asma Jehangir's name should be added to the death list. In frustration, a group attacked Asma's car and attempted to assault her driver, who was quickly whisked away.

'My friends said "We saved your driver but couldn't save your car,"' Asma joked. Protected by her personal bodyguard, she left the court under police escort.

The violence and near riot-like conditions backfired when Prime Minister Bhutto expressed 'shock' at Salamat's sentence. But there were more surprises to come.

I was with Asma Jehangir on the same day that the original charge of blasphemy was withdrawn and Salamat's case collapsed. She told me, 'Don't start celebrating – it's not over. The extremists will want revenge and I am sure that there will be other similar cases. The blasphemy law should be changed.'

Slender and slight, her courage equalled her convictions. She is not a Christian herself, but the Christian community remains in her debt, for she had placed herself in peril by identifying so strongly with them. On one occasion when I met with her, she told me, 'I just learned that my office received a hand-written letter from a fanatic saying that he had been in court with a gun intending to shoot me. The letter said, "I'm going to hunt you down till you are dead. That is my mission."'

Asma told me that Salamat was like any fourteen year old boy. At times, these fantastic events seemed like an adventure to him, yet he was always aware of the terrible risks that he faced.

'When Salamat was told that the court's verdict had condemned him to death by hanging, he said, "I am in God's hands. I am sure that God will give us justice." He seemed shocked yet calm, but when I put my arm around him, he was trembling,' Asma said.

Asma was convinced that the graffiti incident was a trumped-up charge and that Salamat, Manzoor and

Rehmat were innocent. She was equally adamant that the extremists would not be silent for long. Someone must pay.

Later, a highly respected Christian schoolteacher, Cathreen Shaheen, was forced into hiding after repeated death threats. Ann Buwalda worked with top government officials and was able to rescue her.

In another case in 2002, Ayub Masih was freed after spending five years and ten months on Death Row for blasphemy. Once again, Ann was intricately involved with negotiating Ayub's release and she worked closely with the relevant authorities to ensure his safe exit out of Pakistan. Ann told me 'Ayub's acquittal of blasphemy by Pakistan's Supreme Court is a significant judgement and upholds the rule of law. This result preserves the safety and integrity of the legal process in Pakistan for the other Christians currently imprisoned and on Death Row under blasphemy charges.'

With a generous grant from Spring Harvest, we have been able to send practical help to Manzoor Masih's widow and other persecuted Christian families, working through our partner in Pakistan, Joseph Francis of the Centre for Legal Aid, Assistance and Settlement. But the campaign to protect religious freedom isn't over, though our hope is that sense will overrule fanaticism.

10

End Of History 1989

Petru Dugulescu was a dynamic Christian leader with a charismatic personality. His church, in Timisoara, became one of the largest in Romania and his reputation as a preacher placed him in constant demand around the country. He was unstoppable.

Inevitably, he came to the attention of the authorities and one day, in 1985, after completing his theological studies, he was warned by the Romanian secret police to curb his contagious Christian convictions or he'd meet with an 'accident'.

'That'll be the end of you,' the Securitate man hinted.

Sometime after this threat, in September, Petru was driving down a one way street, when a bus, without any passengers, appeared from the opposite direction from a side street, ignored the stop sign, and deliberately rammed his car. The police appeared within seconds, didn't question the driver, but confiscated Petru's driving licence.

Having been injured in the accident, another immediate attempt on his life was thwarted by the quick thinking of a Christian nurse. Petru explained, 'My arm was badly damaged and during the operation to repair the damage, the oxygen tank ran out and the anaesthetist said the hospital had run out of oxygen.'

'A Christian nurse told me later that she was in the operating theatre at the time. She saw that the oxygen was empty and that I was starting to die. She quickly ran to grab another tank, brought it into the operating room, and they hooked it up.'

'Later I spoke to other doctors, and they confirmed my suspicions. Since the accident had failed they were trying to do the job again in the hospital.'

Petru eventually confronted the driver of the bus, who didn't deny that he had been part of a plot to kill him. 'I told him that as a Christian I was compelled to forgive him.'

When the threats and intimidation didn't work, the authorities tried to force him out of town.

Richard Warnes, second left, led one of our first teams into Romania in the eighties. After Ceausescu's downfall, Petru Dugulescu, second from the right, served as an MP in Romania's Parliament and held prayer meetings in Elena Ceausescu's old office.

In England, Brian Mansfield, a member of the Ichthus Fellowship in South London, learned of Petru's predicament, and came up with an inventive idea to gain protection for the Romanian pastor.

Brian had acquired an unwanted x-ray machine and offered it to the hospital in Timisoara. The top medical executive jumped at the chance of getting it. The only condition was that Petru should administer the gift. When the hospital's chief technician asked Petru to handle the transaction, he explained that he had been ordered out of town and hence had no option but to decline. Not wanting to lose the equipment, the medical staff pressured the police to lift the restrictions.

Petru was recognised as a man of influence in the city.

Brian invited me to meet Petru when he visited Britain for medical treatment on his arm, following the 'road accident'. We sat spellbound as Petru revealed what life was really like inside the treacherous and sinister world of Ceausescu's Romania.

It was a criminal offence to use anything stronger than a 40 watt light bulb or to stockpile food. Ambulances would only service adults who could work while the elderly and children were ignored. Christians were routinely tortured and imprisoned, while Bibles were pulped and recycled into toilet paper. Each family was required to produce children on demand, to work for the state, but with severe food shortages, many were abandoned and held in squalid orphanages.

In 1986, we agreed to send practical help to Petru who would then distribute the supplies through his network to the most needy. Howard Taylor worked full time on the project and my friend Dirk Jan Groot's Dorkas Aid International got us started. We hired vans and used church volunteers and arranged between five and fifteen trips into the country annually. Contact was always made at night. If we were caught handing over food or aid, we would have been deported but Petru would have been arrested.

Richard Warnes took a call from the Foreign Office advising us to be cautious. Apparently, the intelligence service had learned that the Romanian authorities were curious about our frequent visits into their country.

The reports out of Romania were shocking, almost unbelievable. We were in a Catch-22 situation. We couldn't reveal everything we knew without endangering Petru and others, and we couldn't publicise our work without revealing the secret life of ordinary Romanians.

It was puzzling. Why had Romania escaped the media's spotlight? Who was responsible for briefing HRH Queen Elizabeth II before she invited the Ceausescus to stay with her at Buckingham Palace, in June 1978, during which visit she bestowed an honorary knighthood on this brutal tyrant?

In *Kiss the Hand You Cannot Bite*, Edward Behr observed that the Queen was reluctant to receive the Romanian dictator.

> The Callaghan government had convinced her that this had been a condition of his coming to Britain in the first place, and that the importance of imminent aircraft and arms sales to Romania made such hospitality mandatory.[1]

In a similar move, President Giscard d'Estaing invited the Ceausescus to France as part of a trade deal involving Renault and the computer firm, Bull. Meanwhile, medals and honours were showered on them from various countries including Denmark, Italy, West Germany, Austria, Belgium and the Netherlands. In the

---

[1] Edward Behr, *Kiss the Hand You Cannot Bite* (London: Penguin, 1992)

United States, President Carter welcomed them, while Richard Nixon became the first American President to visit a Communist nation in Eastern Europe.

Things started to unravel as newspapers reported food riots in Brasov and even Prince Charles expressed 'concern' in 1987 when it was revealed that President Ceausescu planned to bulldoze thousands of villages and demolish historical monuments and churches, some dating back to the thirteenth century.

Another hidden story behind the headlines was simply this: while the Romanian despot was demolishing ancient church buildings, Petru, in Timisoara, was planning to rebuild his church.

After securing planning permission, Petru's ambitious plan was to build a thousand-seater church. Despite tremendous difficulties, the entire congregation paid for and built the structure themselves. It was a remarkable accomplishment. Petru asked if we could help to rewire the building and provide the amplification. With Petru's permission, we secretly filmed the work for a television programme, probably one of the first to be filmed inside Romania.

Trouble was brewing in Timisoara in 1989 when another Christian leader in the city, Laszlo Tokesh, was ordered to leave the city, just as Petru had been earlier. The deadline was set for 15 December 1989. Tokesh's predecessor at the church, Leo Peuker, was known to be a government collaborator, and his superior, Bishop Laszlo Papp, had maintained his position by compromising with the authorities. But when the secret police arrived to evict Tokesh and his wife, they discovered members of his church blocking the entrance of the Hungarian Reformed Church. The vigil grew quickly, as Petru rounded up members from his own church to express solidarity.

The response from ordinary Romanian people must have startled the secret police but no one could have predicted what was ahead.

* * * *

Daniel Gavra stood alongside Petru on the pavement outside Tokesh's small church. He nudged his pastor gently and surreptitiously opened his jacket. Unsure whether the youth was hiding a pistol, Petru's eyes sparkled when he saw a bundle of small candles. Moving covertly, Petru and Daniel passed the candles around and, within a few minutes, the darkness of the Romanian night was transformed by the light from the cluster of candles.

The candlelit vigil continued for a second day, joined by even more people, while the unrest spread to other parts of the city. That night, armoured cars patrolled the streets, as patriotic songs banned by the communists were sung openly, and for the first time voices were raised in protest. The unthinkable was now out in the open, unleashed, and spreading like a shadow across the land.

Before dawn, secret police broke through the vigil and smashed the church door, bundled Laszlo and Edith Tokesh into an unmarked car, and drove into the night.

The news of Tokesh's abduction added fuel to the blazing emotions as thousands took to the streets in unprecedented scenes of protest.

These extraordinary events in Timisoara captured international news headlines but no one could be sure what was happening. Curiously, we were able to telephone Petru's home, and while the international media were reporting that there was a news blackout, we had a hotline to Timisoara.

The media deluged our tiny, one-room office in Richmond, Surrey, and as a result the latest news from Romania was broadcast to the world. It seemed there was only one telephone line left open inside Romania. And it belonged to Petru.

ITV *News at Ten* whisked me down to their London studio for an interview and as I finished one of their reporters told me there was an urgent phone call from the office. It was Robert Day, who whispered conspiratorially, 'Don't say anything but BBC TV *News* have a car outside. They want you to go live on TV news tonight. But they don't want you to tell ITV.'

It was crazy.

Driving home later that night, I became alarmed for Petru and his wife Mary. I knew how Ceausescu's Securitate treated dissidents.

In Timisoara, Petru and his congregation had taken to the streets, part of the thousands of people who sensed they were experiencing an extraordinary moment in history. In Bucharest, on 17 December, the Executive Political Committee condemned the 'mild action' taken by the army in Timisoara and ordered the Securitate to open fire with real bullets. Hundreds of demonstrators were hit, many were killed, including some from Petru's church. Daniel Gavra, who had stood alongside Petru outside Laszlo Tokesh's church, was in the street when bullets smashed into his leg. He fell alongside his girlfriend who was shot dead.

When Petru visited the youth in hospital, he found him in physical pain, grieving, but his spirits were high. Daniel told Petru, 'I lost my friend and I miss her. I lost my leg but I will learn to live with this. After all, I was the one who lit the first candle.'

The Securitate moved swiftly, burying the dead in mass graves and sending other bodies to Bucharest for cremation. Meanwhile, negotiators from Bucharest came to Timisoara to buy time until further troops could be sent to the city in turmoil, but on 19 December the army backed the demonstrators. Ceausescu cut short a visit to Iran and returned the following day to deal with the protest.

Enraged that the protest hadn't been quelled, Ceausescu took charge. He ordered an élite force of trusted troops to crush the rebellion and announced that he would address a mass rally on 21 December. This was to be a fatal mistake, witnessed by the entire country.

The subsequent events, though covered by television cameras, are still shrouded in mystery and intrigue.

Around 12.30pm, Ceausescu appeared on the balcony of the Central Committee building in Bucharest, but the dictator's speech was disrupted and he was forced to leave the podium, amidst growing unease amongst the crowd.

With the country in upheaval, Nicolai and Elena Ceausescu escaped by helicopter, the next day, as street fighting ensued in Bucharest. In an almost comic scene, the couple were picked up by a motorist when their helicopter ran out of fuel. They were caught trying to flee the country, and held at a military base in Tirgoviste, fifty kilometres north of Bucharest. Charged with embezzlement and genocide, the Ceausescus were taken from their improvised courtroom and executed by firing squad on Christmas Day.

In Timisoara, the news that Ceausescu had fled was greeted with tumultuous applause and palpable joy. Thousands took to the streets, while some political leaders took charge in the city's main promenade, Opera Square, the scene where many had fallen. When people in the crowd asked for a Christian message, Petru stepped forward to the main balcony and addressed the crowd.

'I have come to speak to you in the name of God – as you requested. For almost forty years we have been told there is no God. The communists tried to ban God from our hearts and minds, from our schools and our education system. But I am here to speak to you in the name of this God. God exists!'

Inspired by Petru's message, thousands of voices took up his message, 'God exists!' they shouted in unison. 'God is with us!'

Petru continued, 'The communists tried to kill me but I am still alive because God protected me. And I will do everything to bring Pastor Tokesh back to Timisoara. We must have religious freedom here in Timisoara.'

Petru's impromptu sermon continued, interrupted with cheers and applause. He continued, 'This is a historic moment. Let us turn our hearts to God. Please follow me in the Lord's Prayer.'

At that moment, the thousands gathered in the square knelt on the ground, bowed their heads and raised their voices together, in a moment of declared repentance and hope.

Petru's son, Christy, captured the historic event on camera. It was to become a moving tribute to the triumph of faith following decades of oppression. The place where Petru had stood in Opera Square was the very point where Ceausescu had regularly appeared whenever he visited Timisoara.

The international media focused their camera on Timisoara and Romania as these historic events unfolded and for a time everyone was gripped by increased apprehension.

But the professors of Conspiracy Theories were baffled.

Who put the Ceausescus on trial? Who decided they should be executed? The kangaroo court heard that they had deposited $470 million dollars in Swiss banks but how much had been recovered? What really transpired on that fatal day in Bucharest when Ceausescu tried to rally support from the workers? Had he been set up? What happened to his right hand man, army chief General Milea? Had he been shot or had he committed suicide, according to the official record? Had Milea refused to order the troops to shoot at the demonstrators or was he the last man standing in support of the dictator? Was Ceausescu overthrown by spontaneous popular fury, the will of the people, or was this the product of usurpers who wanted to grab power themselves? How had Ion Iliescu, formerly an obedient party loyalist who had been fired by Ceausescu, suddenly emerged out of the chaos at the top of a structured new leadership with a programme in place? What happened to the battalions of Securitate?

And how should we describe events in Romania? Was it a revolution? A riot? An uprising? A *coup d'etat*? A *putsch*?

While the dictionary definition of 'revolution' requires the use of force to overthrow a government or social order, not all Romanians accept that this is what occurred when the communists were overthrown.

Yet everyone agreed that the events in Timisoara were a spontaneous outburst of genuine feeling.

And the spark of light that had ignited change in Timisoara was to spread.

The Cross was Torn from my Neck

While Pier Paulo Pasolini's movies shocked audiences in the west and some demanded that they should be banned, one of his films made a profound impact on a young student in Moscow's Institute of Cinematography. Alexander Ogorodnikov watched an early Pasolini film about the life of Christ and found himself compelled by the central character. The film was like a road sign that was leading to God.

The transformation in Alexander's life was stunning but didn't go unnoticed. Expelled from the film school, he was hounded when he set up the 'Christian Seminar', a discussion group for students. 'Protest became a way of life and also a way of survival in the system of lies,' Alexander explained.

He was arrested in 1978, charged with 'parasitism' – described as the Catch-22 of the criminal code: the victims were prevented from getting a job, then prosecuted for not working. His 'trial' followed a familiar pattern; the public benches were filled in advance by the KGB, so that his friends could not get in. Even his wife and mother were admitted only after lengthy arguments and for only part of the trial. He was beaten with truncheons after being sentenced, and beaten again when, on the way to the labour camp, he asked to see a priest.

Alexander was imprisoned at Perm 36, one of the worst prisons in the Soviet Union, where people such as Anatoly Schcharansky were jailed. He then fell victim to the Soviets' latest vicious trick. He was re-sentenced while still in prison.

Alexander smuggled a letter out of the camp to his mother. Always a gifted writer, it described the pathos and despair that defined his tortured life. Our adoption project in Parliament had already taken action for Alexander but we produced extracts in a poster and circulated it.

The cross was torn from my neck.

I have been thrown into icy cellars in Perm for up to ten days at a time for merely refusing to squat on the floor with my hands clasped behind my back during a search of my cell … in the punishment cell, the weakness brought about by hunger is aggravated by extreme cold. When I spent two months on hunger strike in a punishment cell from December 1983 until February 1984, the ceiling and walls of the cell were entirely covered with ice … my only witnesses were God, and maliciously grinning warders.

The Christian Church has created an immense civilisation and a deep spiritual culture over the past two thousand years but where is the Christian brotherhood, fraternal love, compassion for one's neighbour? It seems to me that the outside Christian world know nothing about my protest fasts, which I have conducted not to secure release from prison. No! The aim was to have a Bible at my disposal, a prayer book and a cross, to enable me to draw faith from the source of Divine Revelation.

Therefore I repeat a request, a decision I reached after much thought and suffering. You must see that death appears to be the only way to end my agony, the only release. I have already committed the moral sin of attempting to commit suicide. I secretly cut my veins, but every time I was discovered, unconscious, but still alive, so they gave me blood transfusions. So, I beg of you again: please appeal to the Presidium of the Supreme Soviet to show me a measure of mercy by ordering my execution by firing squad.

I have spent a total of 659 days on hunger strike to protest against their refusal to let me have a Bible and a prayer book … I do not know whether there was a Christian anywhere who expressed support for me during those days, and it frightens me to think that maybe there wasn't.

Only the full glare of publicity can alter my fate, and that of others in the same situation. Only this can restrain the hands of those who are otherwise free to wreak whatever atrocities they will, with us ...

What awaits me now? Only God knows. I am kept in a cell with violent criminals, most of them imprisoned for murder... one of them, who murdered two people, has openly threatened to kill me. He is awaiting execution by firing squad and brags that as far as he is concerned, he may as well be shot for killing three people, as for killing two ... It looks as though I will be sent to a camp for hardened criminals where I will be totally at the mercy of the camp administration ... my only hope is the mercy of God.

They even forbid me to pray, and my cross has been torn from my neck on thirty occasions ... is it not possible to appeal to western churchmen to take it upon themselves to ensure that I receive a Bible and prayer book, even if they be in English, French or German? Will not the universal church say at least a word in support of one of her persecuted sons – errant and sinful, but still her son?

The letter created a stir. Even Bernard Levin, *The Times'* celebrated columnist, dedicated a feature to him. Levin bluntly demanded action: In Christ's name, speak up.

The publicity and pressure worked. At a summit with Mrs Thatcher, President Gorbachev declared that Alexander was to be released. Everyone in the human rights circle breathed a collective sigh of relief. But behind the scenes a personal tragedy was awaiting him. The cruellest deceit was the final one. Convinced by the KGB that Alexander would never be released, and told that he would die in prison, his beloved wife, Irina, remarried just days before the prison gates opened and he walked out a free man.

Unlike other dissidents, Alexander chose to stay in Russia. We became friends over the next few years and provided some assistance to help him set up a political party, the Christian Democratic Union.

Towards the end of the year, newspaper reports warned of widespread food shortages, even famine, in Moscow. Late one night, the phone rang and I recognised Alexander's soft lilting voice.

'People are dying,' Alexander said. 'Old people are facing great hardships. Can you help?'

Alexander wanted to open a food kitchen to feed the poor and destitute. Together with Dirk Jan Groot, (from Dorkas Aid International), we produced ration books with coupons. People in the west would buy the ration books for Russians to use the coupons. The idea caught on. The *Sun* newspaper backed our campaign and the recently formed Movement for Christian Democracy pledged their support. Within days, David Alton arranged a meeting with Soviet Ambassador Zamyatin

Alexander Ogorodnikov unloads the missing supplies destined for our food kitchen in Moscow.

Photo: *The Times*

who guaranteed the use of an Aeroflot transport plane to fly our food supplies to Moscow.

Attending the meeting with us were representatives from the Women's Campaign for Soviet Jewry. We emerged somewhat dazed. After years of campaigning, we had now been inside the Embassy, face to face with people who had been the focus of our protests.

The media backed our campaign and the authorities at Stansted Airport were fantastic, while Bill Gribbin, the writer, kept a watchful eye on the supplies at a warehouse nearby.

Several tons of food piled in with additional donations by Milupa and United Biscuits and the first plane load was loaded and airborne on Boxing Day, December 26. We were ecstatic. So was Alexander when we phoned him with the news.

Then the trouble started.

When Alexander went to the airport to take delivery of the food he faced a familiar refrain. No one knew anything. What food? No food was on the flight. Gatwick Airport's shipping agents, Gatwick Handling, confirmed that the food was on board. Express Service, the Soviet freight forwarding company, which volunteered to process the gifts said that the aircraft arrived fully loaded but the flight manifest made no mention of food for Moscow. Soviet authorities were adamant. There was no food on the plane.

The story hit the media and *The Times* carried a front page report. 'Moscow-bound food cargo goes missing'. Another headline declared 'Food for Russia disappears'.

With thirty tons due into the warehouse, concern was mounting that our project would be discredited and supplies would dry up.

The Soviets blamed us. They told the press that our food hadn't been labelled. The food could be anywhere. How do we know?

Riding to the rescue, Bill Gribbin arrived breathless in our office with photos he had taken, showing the cargo being loaded on to the plane. The photos hit the newspapers, keeping us on the front page. One photo clearly stated 'Moscow Aid/Jubilee Campaign/Immediate Clearance'.

The photos in the media produced a Houdini-like impact in Moscow. Suddenly our food was found. Still, the local authorities stubbornly refused to hand it over, but after David telephoned the Ambassador, the game was up.

In the final days of the crumbling communist empire, Moscow had become the venue for a brutal turf war. The communists clung to power, refusing to give up control of lucrative under-the-counter deals, creating trouble for the genuine liberal and new wave politicians who were desperately trying to seize the moment. Edging nearer were the notorious Mafia-like gangs, determined to claim a piece of the action. Their policy was simple. They ruled by the gun and would shoot anyone who got in the way. Alexander walked a tightrope amidst this maze of violence, making dangerous enemies along the way.

The independently-run Moscow City Council signed a contract with Alexander and us for the food kitchen to be opened near the city centre but a local communist boss, Vladimir Michailov, realised its prime location could be financially lucrative. He launched a campaign of intimidation and local thugs disrupted the building and the plans for renovation.

Despite all the threats, history was made in April 1991, when the first free food kitchen in Moscow opened its doors to the poor and elderly and several hundred people were fed. Each one through the door held a coupon from the ration books that people in Britain and Holland had purchased.

But the pressure intensified. The electricity was turned off and some food perished in the freezer. Meanwhile tyres were slashed on a vehicle that we and the Movement for Christian Democracy had donated to be used in the distribution of food. Alexander had strong local support and when he held a prayer meeting in the building, the event was filmed by Moscow television.

In Britain, the political battle continued as David Alton pressed the Soviet Ambassador for guarantees that Alexander would not be harmed and that the food kitchen could remain open. Finally, the Council ruled that alternative premises would have to be found before Alexander was evicted. It was a compromise but was the best outcome we could have hoped for.

In Moscow, something was stirring. There was a feeling in the air. Danger and hope. And excitement. People like Alexander were taking the first few steps of freedom, with no one knowing where it would lead. While words like *glasnost* and *perestrokia* were entering the textbooks, defining a moment in history, we were caught up with real people in true life situations. No one had prepared us for a time such as this. No one was sure what to do next. All we could do was take one step at a time.

The eruption happened in Moscow and television cameras captured courageous protestors who shielded the Russian Parliament building with their bodies. The army were called in and tanks rolled. The world held its breath.

At midnight, Alexander telephoned me with this message:

> When I heard news of the coup, I prepared myself for prison. The KGB warned us that we were an illegal organisation and our telephone line had been cut from the first day of the coup.

Initially about thirty people gathered around the Russian Parliament building. But as the news spread, more arrived. It was amazing. There were old women besides punks and rockers. Young people without any political agenda. A rock band played music. Even criminals turned up because everyone understood that our freedom was in peril.

There was such an electric atmosphere among the people. It was absolutely unbelievable. I was so moved. I began to cry like a child.

We were among the first to take action. We did this against the direct orders of the communists. We published the latest news and stuck leaflets on the walls.

In the food kitchen we prepared food that you sent us to feed the 'resistance'. Our team worked day and night. We made several tons of sandwiches. We drove to the square in your van and were there all night, walking and talking, among the people.

It was dangerous. Bullets were flying over my head. A bullet struck the van. It was a time of extraordinary courage. I saw a woman with children in her arms block a tank with her body. We stopped several soldiers and appealed to them. 'Turn back!' we cried. At 3am one morning I talked with the chief of a military unit. 'Don't shoot the people,' I pleaded. 'Don't shed the blood of our Russian people.'

When the coup crumbled, there was such joy. We knew the communist system was doomed. We knew it was dead. But now we were witnessing its collapse. It was like a miracle.

Flowers in the Ukraine

Mikhail Gorbachev's radical policies caused tremors throughout the communist world and led to the collapse of the Berlin wall and the release of religious and political prisoners in the Soviet Union and Eastern Europe. But the Ukraine remained under the control of the authorities, a country that Gorbachev's *glasnost* couldn't reach.

Like the early church, the Ukrainian Catholic Church, numbering five million people, was forced to go underground and worship secretly. Illegal since 1946, we launched a campaign to seek its legalisation, working with the Ukrainian Church in Britain and in the Vatican. In 1989, David Alton visited the Ukraine. BBC TV's *Newsnight* broadcast a filmed diary of his journey and the *Independent* newspaper reprinted his diary, titled 'Flowers in the Ukraine'.

Arriving at the Ukrainian border town of Mostiska on a train from Przemysl, it had just turned the witching hour. With two friends from Jubilee Campaign, we had our journey toward Lvov abruptly interrupted.

Up stepped half a dozen Soviet officials who ordered us to disembark with our luggage. This was the friendly face of Vladimir Shcherbitsky's reception committee – Gorbachev sacked him two days after we left. For the next four hours, long after our train had departed with the rest of its passengers, the bureaucrats dissected our luggage and scoured our visas and passports.

Subversive and seditious materials, such as a biography of Basil Hume, the writings of medieval English mystic Julian of Norwich and, to the delight of my local paper, a copy of the *Liverpool Echo*, were too hot to handle. All were carefully documented and receipts issued. Could we have a cup of tea? Nyet.

At 4am we were finally allowed to board an empty train – circa 1930, exquisite rolling stock, hard wooden seats – and continued our journey east. With two and a half hours travel ahead of us, I could have read the little book, entitled *Perestroika*, handed to me by the head of the reception committee, had it not been written in German. No doubt to compensate for my confiscated Basil Hume they also gave me a Lenin on the Great Socialist Revolution – in English. Surely he didn't have all this trouble on his train ride to Petrograd.

In Lvov we met Ivan Hel, who was released two years ago, in 1987, after 15 years incarceration. He is the leader of the movement to legalise the Ukrainian Catholic Church suppressed by Stalin in 1946. His first brush with the KGB was in 1961 and he was held at Mordovia Prison and then at Perm. Temperatures plunged way below zero, he was kept half naked and fed infrequently. For three years, letters from his wife, Maria, and his daughter were not permitted.

After supper at their two-room flat came a traditional late-night knock on the door. Checking out the guest list were two senior members of Shcherbitsky's militia. No wonder Hel says that perestroika is a joke in the Ukraine.

Hel is in the mould of Lech Walesa, the force at the centre of the Solidarity movement in Poland, combining deeply held faith with shrewd political judgement. The national-ities' question for him is first about legalisation of the banned church but also about sovereignty and self-determination for the Ukraine's 51 million people.

Hel is part of the Popular Front, which is pressing for political reform and he is involved in establishing the new Christian Democratic movement. He quotes Khvyloviy, the 1930s Ukrainian poet, enthusiastically: 'Away from Moscow, towards Europe.' This potent cock-tail of faith and politics brought out a quarter of a million people on to Lvov's streets. Many attended an open-air mass, held in the shadow of two Catholic churches closed by Stalin.

What was remarkable about these buildings was the flowers laid on their steps every day since 1946. At the former Armenian Church, the statue of Christ had been decapitated. Someone had tied a crown of thorns to the rail-ing. Shcherbitsky's men regularly remove it and, just as remarkably, another appears in its place.

Flowers are an abiding memory of my time in the Ukraine. At the makeshift banned memorial to the Ukraine's national poet, Taras Sheuchenko, people queued to lay flowers alongside his photograph. This spot doubles as the local Hyde Park Corner and the focal point for national fervour. The once-banned yellow and blue twelfth century Ukrainian flag fluttered as a young bride and groom came to make their vows and swear allegiance to their country, the Ukraine, not the Soviet Union.

Perhaps Shcherbitsky's lasting monument will be Chernobyl.

A Ukrainian priest, Fr Mikhaylo Havryliv was sent to Chernobyl, the world's worst nuclear power accident, as a punishment, to clear contaminated radioactive debris. His crime was to openly celebrate the sacraments. His bishop, Pavlo Vasylyk, himself a survivor of 18 years imprisonment, told me that this typified the cruelty and barbarism of this relic of the Brezhnev era. Perhaps it is even worse than that.

Every church building belonging to the Ukrainian Catholic Church was seized in 1946, the church hierarchy imprisoned, and church members became outlaws. Yet, just as the flowers kept appearing outside closed church buildings, new generations of believers were drawn into the illegal church and secret services continued. And gradually, the church has re-emerged from its catacombs.

The Empire Crumbles

1989 was a pivotal year that demonstrated we were living in momentous times. The world around us was changing.

In China, students had challenged the state in a memorable demonstration, occupying Tiananmen Square. Retribution followed as tanks and soldiers cleared the path with ruthless efficiency, leaving many dead.

The enduring image of that moment was captured by a Magnum photographer, Stuart Franklin, showing one man who confronted a row of tanks and for a fleeting moment brought the onslaught to a halt.

'Why are you here?' the individual yelled at the anonymous steel tank. 'You have done nothing but create misery. My city is in chaos because of you.'

Six months after this epic struggle, people again took to the streets in Timisoara, and within weeks, the scholars were struggling to comprehend the cataclysmic changes that were rattling through the communist world.

While historic moments aren't always obvious and don't come with road signs, the winds of change were

A secret Christmas service in the snow in the Ukraine. Fr Mikhaylo Havryliv (right) was forced to clear radioactive waste from Chernobyl without adequate protection, as punishment for performing his priestly duties.

wafting through the communist strongholds. Political and military systems that had withstood several decades were crumbling. And television cameras were capturing the moment.

The tyrants in our modern age of mediaism had carefully manipulated the press. Acts of aggression and oppression happened under cover of darkness. Somehow, the power of the image – both still photographs and moving pictures – imbued a sense of authority and significance to the event. Stories with moving pictures made it on to television, while events without camera coverage left little impact upon the masses. In this way, the masters of the communist world had been able to rewrite history, sometimes literally airbrushing rebels from photographs, making them non-persons, who existed only in the memory of eye-witnesses and an inner circle. The collapse of communism provided memorable visuals and thereby contributed to its own significance, with the cracks in the monolith appearing live on television.

The word *glasnost* became synonymous with the mammoth changes occurring within the sprawling empire of the Soviet Union, with Mikhail Gorbachev the ring master. Almost single-handedly, he tried to stop the runaway train of tyranny while the western world watched goggle-eyed at the witness of the secular miracle. Like a circus showman under the spotlight of the international arena's omnipotent media machine, Mr Gorbachev conducted acts of amazement, while the door swung open providing us with a fascinating glimpse inside a society best known for its secrecy. At the time no one could predict whether the '*glasnost* express' would turn out to be a toy train made of cardboard and Sellotape.

There were many sceptics. The poet, Irina Ratushinskya, told me that she considered her release from labour camp to be a 'show' but the tumultuous turn of global events was beyond everyone's imagination. Even the CIA's billion dollar budget hadn't predicted the fall of communism and the changes were so significant that some considered the end of history was upon us and that we were on the brink of a new phase of human society and history.

As historians were seeking iconic moments to understand the changes, many were turning to dissidents, intellectuals, artists and Christians for the moral authority to direct the way forward. Ironically, totalitarian regimes were undermined by individual act of defiance, acting out Alexander Solzhenitsyn's command that 'one word of truth outweighs the world.'

Poland's Adam Michnik wrote from prison, 'You score a victory not when you win power but when you remain faithful to yourself.' Throughout the communist world, just attending church was an act of protest. Alexander Ogorodnikov observed, 'Protest became a way of life and also a way of survival in the system of lies.'

But the towers of communism that challenged faith-filled intellectuals and believers would totter and eventually tumble, and it would be Alexander Solzhenitsyn, a decade earlier, who would write what would become the final epitaph: 'No matter how formidably communism bristles with tanks and rockets, no matter what success it attains in seizing the planet, it is doomed never to vanquish Christianity.'

Hideout on Pirate Island

Ten years after David launched Jubilee Campaign in Parliament, we were making plans to publicise the anniversary when the phone rang.

'A young Christian family have escaped from China and are hiding in Hong Kong. We need to get them out. Is there anything you can do?'

The newspaper headlines summarised the context. For the first time ever, Britain was about to hand over a colony, once known as Pirate Island, to a communist state at midnight on 30 June 1997. Seven thousand journalists flooded into Hong Kong as the electronic media turned this extraordinary moment in history into a unique global event.

But behind the scenes, a dramatic story was unfolding and I sensed the urgency as we delved deeper. With every passing hour, I was certain that my time should be spent investigating this story. The heart of Jubilee was to serve and it was appropriate that our publicity plans should be superseded by the drama in Hong Kong and the question: What could we do to help Bob and Heidi Fu and their six week old son, hiding in Hong Kong?

Our long-range plans were hindered by contradictory communication, delayed by the different time zones involved. The US State Department told our American office that the Fu family were on their way to a Nordic country but when we checked with Hong Kong, Bob knew nothing about it.

Newspaper reports disturbed us further. A new law forbade anyone without official documents to remain in Hong Kong after the hand-over. This news increased the psychological pressure on the couple. If we were going to help, we had just twenty-one days left before the hand-over to Communist China.

Armed with an appeal from David Alton to his friend, Chris Patten, the Governor of Hong Kong, I set off on the twelve-hour flight, relieved that an hour before my departure, confirmation had come through that I had a bed in the city, even more crammed with tourists for the event.

The story in Hong Kong was inspiring and alarming.

Bob and Heidi had been leaders in the student move-ment in China in the late eighties and were among the radicals who protested in Tiananmen Square. Bob graduated in International Politics from the People's University and then taught English to the children of senior officials at the Communist Party School in Beijing. Heidi studied philosophy but also taught at a middle school in Shandong for two years. As prominent intel-lectuals, they were clearly destined for influential positions, but in the aftermath of the Tiananmen Square massacre, disillusioned with the system, they came to personal faith. Working with the underground church they set up an effective training centre and became key leaders in the church.

Problems emerged, in 1996, when their teaching pro-gramme was exposed. Retribution was swift. They were arrested and jailed for two months. Following their release, Bob was dismissed from his job, Heidi was told that she would not graduate, and they were given two months to vacate their apartment. Surveillance increased as local police pressured them to reveal their foreign con-tacts. A sympathetic insider warned them that they would be arrested shortly.

Convinced that they should leave, Bob and Heidi escaped from China – a story in itself – and went into hiding in Hong Kong.

Assuming that they would leave for the west within days, they packed their suitcases and sat in a room, waiting. But days turned to weeks, and eventually, months. Almost a year passed. Their case had become unnecessarily com-plicated, tangled with red tape, bureaucratic squabbles and misinformation, leaving their situation gridlocked.

In April 1997, Daniel was born to Heidi and Bob in the Prince of Wales Hospital in Hong Kong. What should have been the happiest time of their life turned into a nightmare, but Bob and Heidi remained calm. 'We rely on God alone,' Bob told me, when I visited their flat, two hours after I arrived in Hong Kong, on a rainy afternoon in June. 'We know he has a plan for our lives and accept whatever happens to us as God's will. We felt God was guiding us to take the dramatic step of escaping from China. We're in his hands.'

Within a few hours together, we became exceptionally close. For me, this was no longer a campaign and they weren't names on paper. Bob and Heidi, and little Daniel, had become friends and I was determined to do everything I could to help them.

David Alton's letter to Chris Patten prised open the diplomats' inner chamber as I started to unravel the difficulties. The first hurdle was dis-information. They had no chance of getting into a 'Nordic country', as the US State Department had insisted. Sweden had already refused them. It was unsettling to hear some diplomats think that their case could still be worked on after the hand-over. As Bob and Heidi were facing arrest in China, staying on would leave them trapped in Hong Kong at the mercy of the Chinese authorities. It seemed that, unofficially, Bob and Heidi were marked out as a test case to see how China would treat dissidents. I was determined that the politicians should find another guinea pig for this bizarre experiment. The western diplomats weren't prepared to be questioned and didn't respond positively to my challenges, but there was little they could do. As a result of David Alton's letter to Chris Patten, the Governor of Hong Kong had extended me a hand of welcome.

The flurry of meetings, faxes and telephone calls escalated over the next few days as I averaged three hours sleep a night, desperately trying to find help. Someone.

Anyone. Washington. London. Copenhagen. Paris. Even Tokyo. My phone bill ran into telephone numbers.

Meanwhile in Washington, during the final count-down before the hand-over of Hong Kong to China, Ann and her team in the US began a concentrated series of phone calls to numerous Congressional offices and initiated direct legal intervention. On Monday, the US State Department's position was 'We know one thing – they're not coming here.' By Friday, the same official stated 'We know one thing – they are coming here.'

The lobbying had worked and it ended just as it had begun – with a telephone call.

'It's the breakthrough we've been praying for!' Bob could hardly contain his excitement.

Forty-eight hours before the deadline, their visa was approved and they rushed to Kai Tak Airport to start a thirty hour journey, with two stopovers, ending in North Carolina. Bob's message on our answer-phone said it all, 'We made it out of Hong Kong! Your visit was a turning point in our case. Thank you!'

Back at the office, we also made it. The team pulled together, while I was in Hong Kong, and produced a review of the past decade's campaigns.

I returned from Hong Kong, exhausted but exhilarated. Working on Bob and Heidi's case had inspired me in a fresh way and convinced me that I had made the right decision by not staying in the office but leaving immediately for the danger zone of the diplomatic terrain. It was also a vivid reminder of just why we started Jubilee in the first place.

11

They Shoot Children, Don't They?

When our friends, such as Petru in Romania and Alexander in Russia, asked for practical help, existing groups offered meagre support, if any. We felt compelled to respond but I was cautious about plunging ahead and setting up a charity. I didn't think the world was waiting for yet another organisation and I sought advice from a few people. In one memorable conversation, Peter Benenson, the founder of Amnesty International, a good friend to our family, told me, 'Don't duplicate in a small way what another organisation is doing in a big way. Don't become a small version of a bigger organisation merely copying what they do. Make your time count. Use your money wisely. Keep your commitment dynamic and personal to a specific group. Try to work where others aren't involved. In that way if you stop, you will be missed.'

It made fantastic sense and I followed the advice as if it was a guiding star advancing through the unfathomable universe. In time, Jubilee Action emerged as a human rights charity, with its mandate enshrined in the challenge: bringing hope, changing lives.

Reports from Romania shook the world as television coverage exposed Ceausescu's devastating brutality and the living hell of Romania's orphans. When the *Sunday Times* reported that we were among the first to take supplies into Romania we received widespread support, including a message from Olivia Harrison, who wanted to make a donation. I suggested that she visit Romania herself. She was so moved by the experience that she decided to donate more than money. She set up the Romanian Angel Appeal, drawing in Elton John and the wives of the other Beatles and invited me to serve as a trustee of the new organisation.

Olivia's magnetism, energy and profile ensured the issue stayed on the front page, as the *Daily Mail* carried a six week series of articles with our address for people to send money. The excitement increased when George Harrison drew in Bob Dylan, Tom Petty and Jeff Lynne (the fantastic Travelling Wilburys) and released *Nobody's Child* with all the profits going to the charity. An album

Nobody's child: just one of Romania's orphans.
Photo: Howard Taylor

was rushed out with contributions from artists, including Elton John, Eric Clapton, Van Morrison and Stevie Wonder, among others.

The album, and subsequent publicity, raised over $2 million and our plans to see an effective programme to refurbish orphanages became a reality. Jubilee continued a strong partnership with the Romanian Angel Appeal to seek long-term improvements in the treatment and health care for children and HIV positive children. It was a thrilling moment in time and yet another turning point for us.

* * * *

Olivia introduced me to Aninha Capaldi, the vivacious Brazilian wife of Jim Capaldi, drummer and lyricist with the rock group, Traffic, and together we discussed the phenomenon of the world's street children and wondered if there was anything we could do. At the time, the concept of 'street children' was relatively unknown, while statistics were running wild, with unconfirmed reports that there were a hundred million street children worldwide. We observed that children were classified as follows:

- Children on the Street: The largest group, this comprises children who work in the street, with fairly strong family contact, and whose income is essential to the survival of their family.
- Children of the Street: With little family contact, these include runaways; abused, alienated children from deprived and poverty stricken families who are unable to maintain normal family units. They sleep in doorways, alleys, under bridges, in railway stations; survive by begging and petty theft: while some strive

for educational standards and employment, relatively few succeed without assistance. Drifting into crime, drug gangs and prostitution, these children are victims that can't escape this vicious spiral of violence and destitution.

- Children in the Street: The smallest group covers orphans and abandoned children whose parents could have died from war, illness or have simply been unable to look after their child because of family circumstances. These children live on their own without family relationships.
- Recyclers: Although not a formal categorisation, recyclers survive on the rubbish dumps or discarded items they find on the streets. The children of recyclers spend day and night on the streets within the family groups. They survive by selling papers and materials, and in some countries, live on rubbish dumps or on

An abandoned child's body found on a beach in Rio de Janeiro.   Photo: *Opovo*, Jubilee

the streets. They are seen as a marginalised group, the scum of society. In Colombia, the Procuraduria identified two types: those who have a room and may own a horse and cart (known as 'Zorros'). Others live on the streets, sleeping in either a house of cardboard boxes or in the carts they use for collecting the rubbish.

With news that at least three children a day were being killed in Rio de Janeiro, Aninha's hometown, we decided Brazil was the place to start. During our two week visit, we met with street children, media and government officials, as well as the promoter of 'Rock in Rio', the biggest rock event in the world. Everyone knew the streets were dangerous and that many died in drug deals, inter-gang warfare and criminal violence, but dark rumours persisted that death squads were executing

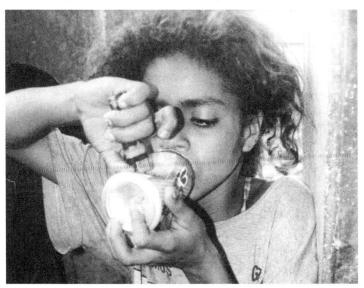

Life on the streets.   Photo: Matt Roper

children in a campaign to 'clean up the streets'. Equally disturbing was the apparent inability of the authorities to investigate these child murders and to order the prosecution of the perpetrators of violence against children.

The breakdown of traditional family units had driven children from their homes and on to the streets, while a huge surge from the country to the city was causing considerable urban turmoil. This trend has continued globally with predictions that by the year 2030, for the first time in our history, 60 per cent of the world's people will live in cities.

In 1950, there was just one city with a population of more than ten million – New York. In 2015 there will be twenty-one mega-cities, and the number of urban areas with populations between five and ten million will escalate from seven to thirty-seven. Observers tell us that this growth will occur primarily in developing countries, those least equipped to provide transportation, housing, water and sewers. Asia and Africa, now more than two-thirds rural, will be half urban by 2025. With the emergence of an increasing number of mega-cities, the inherent social problems are doomed to increase. The predictions are that the number of abandoned children will double, only contributing further to the sense of injustice and inequality amongst the world's poor that has driven extremists within their midst to seek violent solutions to the problem. With more than half the world's peoples moving from the rural areas to the cities, how they adjust to their new habitat will define the twenty-first century.

* * * *

On the flight back from Brazil we drafted a letter of protest that said simply: Stop Killing Street Children.

Signed by George, Olivia, Jim, Aninha and their friends, the signatures captured a glittering array of personalities, including Sir Paul McCartney, Ringo Starr, Phil Collins, Emerson Fittipaldi and Richard Branson.

I knew that this was a significant development but how could we use it to the greatest impact? Our objective was to maintain control over the story, to determine how it was used, so that the emphasis of street children was not lost, to ensure that the celebrities who suppor-ted our campaign weren't compromised, and that Jubilee's role wasn't eroded. Understanding how the press works and charting a course through the media jungle can be tricky.

While we were wondering how to secure the story within the stronghold of Fleet Street, two of Britain's top journalists were making plans to work on a story about street children in Brazil.

Chief foreign correspondent Daniel McGrory and photographer John Downing were award-winning journalists who had maintained the *Daily Express*' reputation as a major news force. John had recently been awarded the Order of the British Empire for his work and the editor of the *Express* told him that, as a reward, he could do any story he wanted. John chose to cover the issue of street children.

When we made contact, their response was immediate. 'That's just the issue we want to cover!'

With Daniel and John at the helm, we achieved all our objectives.

The *Express* splashed the story across the front page, with a banner heading showing a child in the cross hairs of a gun sight, depicting children at risk. The story ran for four days and the letter of appeal, championed by the Harrisons and the Capaldis, was used, with Jubilee's address featured in every issue.

This was probably the first time that the British media had given the issue such prominent coverage and the story would have a ripple effect all over the world. It would help to put the plight of street children on the international agenda.

I wanted to harness our Parliamentary supporters beyond a one-off meeting but wasn't sure how to drive the intangible idea forward. While waiting in the hall-way of an ante room in the House of Commons one rainy afternoon, I picked up a leaflet that had been dropped by the occupants of an early session. It revealed that a group of jazz enthusiasts met regularly within the House of Commons. At first it was amusing. I imagined a smoky room late at night filled with MPs and their cohorts bopping to the rhythms that came off the river-boats down the Mississippi through New Orleans and Memphis with the beat that had been carried from the slave ships from Africa.

After the amusement passed, I was intrigued. If jazz fans met regularly in the Commons, could we have a Parliamentary Group dedicated to street children?

There were some immediate hurdles to overcome. Who would handle the administrative backup? The problem was solved when we suggested that Jubilee would serve as its secretariat. How could we choose a chairman without displaying any political bias? Easy, we'd have three chairmen.

David Alton moved through the political maze and eased the passage for the formation of the group, recruiting Labour MP Nigel Griffiths and Conservative MP Ian Bruce, as co-chairmen. Olivia and Aninha pulled in Jimmy Nail, Wimbledon Football Club Chairman Sam Hammam, among others, and the All Party Parliamentary Group on Street Children was launched in the House of Commons. It was a stirring moment as a powerful forum was established within the structures of Parliament, dedicated to using the political system to defend the rights of vulnerable children of the streets.

The Brazilian authorities were doing what they could but the problems were widespread. To maintain the pressure, we linked up with the *Daily Mirror's* chief foreign correspondent, Anton Antonovich, on another investigation, and again the story was given massive coverage in 1998. Veteran musician Peter Kirtley read the *Mirror* and was outraged and moved. He wrote and recorded *Little Children*, the evocative and moving story of children on the streets, with the active involvement of Sir Paul McCartney. Radio stations plugged it and even Virgin's Megastore on London's Oxford Street put the catchy song on its playlist.

The Boy I Never Knew

On our first night in Brazil, Aninha took us to a small downtown arts cinema to see a documentary about the transitory – and dangerous – life of children on Rio's streets. Some of the street kids featured in the film were at the cinema and their raucous cheers announced their arrival on screen.

Aninha had met the street boys the previous night and over the next few days we got to know some of them. Anderson, warm, lovable, carried his books carefully, determined to complete school. Luciano, boisterous, loud, pinched and hugged me, grabbed my camera and took several shots from precarious angles. And Juanito, tall, gangly, a loner, reserved, often remote; in retrospect, someone I never got close to.

It was evident that each of them had done time at the dark end of Rio's mean streets. Coming to the Sao

Martinho Shelter, a Catholic charity in the city, had been a turning point in their lives. The boys were tough, streetwise, yet vulnerable, tender, like young adults who had bypassed childhood. Almost everyone wanted the same thing: a home. Someone to care for them. To finish school. Get a job. Settle down.

Juanito wanted to be a cook and spent much of his time in the shelter's kitchen. But he had problems fitting in and may have had learning difficulties. When asked what his ambition was, he replied wistfully, 'To get a girlfriend but I'm too ugly.'

Juanito was one of the boys selected to perform for John Major, the only Head of State to visit a children's shelter, Sao Martinho, during the Earth Summit in Rio. Sometime during the festivities, Juanito drew close, oblivious to protocol, extended his hand and in a flash of

Aninha Capaldi with John Major at the Sao Martinho shelter.   Photo: *The Times*

spontaneity, Mr Major clasped the palm of the boy who lived on the streets.

That moment was to become a tragic television epitaph. Four months after the encounter, Juanito was dead. He was shot in the head and in the chest near his sister's home in the *Favela de Nova Iguacu*. We pressed for an investigation and eventually were told that Juanito might have inadvertently annoyed a local gangster in the slums. The suspected killer died soon after in mysterious circumstances.

I have often reflected on Mr Major's visit and what must have been Juanito's proudest moment. For once in his life, he reached out and someone was there to take his hand. Tragically, it was not always to be that way. He was acquainted with the violence of the streets and though not personally involved, one day was eventually overcome by it.

Mr Major was mobbed by the street kids at Sao Martinho and genuinely moved by the experience. Aninha was on hand and served as his interpreter, and when he asked her if there was something more that he could do, she was ready.

Aninha told the Prime Minister that girls on the street faced harrowing ordeals as they struggled to survive. Some lost their childhood, others their lives. Thrust into a vicious adult world, girls as young as eleven and twelve had turned up at Sao Martinho in desperate circumstances. Some were pregnant with nowhere to go, others were on the run, after falling into petty crime. Tragically, they were turned away as Sao Martinho had no facilities for them, and neither did anyone else. There was no shelter in the city that cared specially for girls.

'I'll see what I can do,' he told Aninha.

True to his word, Mr Major made finances available for a house to be purchased for street girls and it immediately provided shelter for about twenty girls. The Girls Home became our major project in Brazil and with us, Aninha worked hard to raise funds to keep it going. For the girls, it was a dream come true.

When Princess Diana wrote and told us of her interest in the home and indicated that she would get involved, we were thrilled. Following her tragic death, we named the home 'The Princess Diana Home for Street Girls' in her memory.

Many years have passed. Things have changed. I don't know if we ever got over the news of the falling of Juanito. In a way, Jubilee's mission to protect and care for children at risk unfolded more fully after our visit to Brazil. Over the past decade, Aninha Capaldi has emerged as a champion of street children. We often reflect on that first night at the movies in Rio when she introduced me to Anderson, Luciano and Juanito.

After the film, I bought chocolates for everyone as we stood in the cinema's lobby. Luciano immediately snapped his bar in half and handed it to me. I was reluctant to accept it but he forced the chocolates on me in a move that was both instinctive and affectionate. We shared a moment in time, both exchanging gifts and each grateful to the other for the experience. But the gifts were different. Mine was probably superficial, purchased with a few coins, and could be replicated with ease.

The character of life is comprised of such moments and the poignancy of the encounter has never left me.

12

Human Wrongs

With David Alton's help, Jubilee Campaign developed an unrivalled Parliamentary network in Westminster, and in time this extended to European Parliament, while Ann Buwalda secured strong political support in Washington. Each year we returned to the United Nations Human Rights Commission to raise cases of persecuted Christians and children at risk. Meanwhile, our fund-raising skills were dismal and our administrative foundation neglected.

The Dying Rooms of China

Dr Stephen Mosher was the first American social scientist student to enter China, after President Carter normalised relations with that country in 1979. He spent a year in South China, living in a country village studying family life, and witnessed how women who were six or even nine months' pregnant were rounded up if they refused abortions. Their pregnancies were terminated in bloody conditions and some women were compulsorily sterilised. Dr Mosher's reports provided firsthand evidence of the abuse of women and first alerted the world to the vicious nature of China's population control policy.

China is the world's largest nation with 21 per cent of the population – 1.2 billion people, but only 7 to 10 per cent of the suitable land for cultivation. With growth at 15 per cent, 160 million more people would be added to the population within the decade. In 1971, the Chinese government aggressively promoted family planning and eight years later launched the controversial 'one child policy'. This introduced rewards and penalties to induce couples to limit their family to one child.

For thousands of years, Chinese cultural tradition dictated that every family must have a son or risk dishonouring their ancestors. Fireworks celebrate the birth of a boy, but girl babies are ignored. Abandoning children is illegal and carries stiff penalties, but parents seem willing to take the risk because they don't want to waste their only chance of a child on a girl.

Left by roadsides, riverbanks and in railway stations, many abandoned children die of exposure, others are picked up by gangs and used as beggars. State-run orphanages are under-funded and understaffed, and in some during the mid-1990s, the death rate for babies could be as high as one in five.

In 1995, independent film makers Brian Woods and Kate Blewett decided to investigate newspaper reports that baby girls were being abandoned in China, and sometimes left to die in state orphanages. They travelled covertly and visited over a dozen orphanages in five provinces. Nothing prepared them for the discovery they would make.

Brian said later, 'There were times when we just broke down in the hotel afterwards. We were seeing some terrible things.'

They filmed baby girls in dirty soiled clothes tied to wicker chairs, their legs splayed. Underneath were potties and old washing bowls. Without toys or distractions, they rocked back and forward all day.

With Kate, Brian spoke movingly as they showed us photographs of the harrowing visit.

> This little girl was two years old. She sat tied to a potty bench all day long. Because she had a deformed lip, she was tormented by the older inmates.
>
> We filmed as a seven year old boy head butted this young girl. Four times her tiny body shook with the impact. Tired of the game, he rubbed his head and moved away. She didn't even cry out – at two, she had already learned that no one would come to her aid.
>
> The most shocking orphanage we visited lay, ironically, just twenty minutes from one of the five-star international hotels that heralded China's emergence from economic isolation.
>
> A disabled girl took me by the hand and pulled me into a darkened room. She led me to a pile of crumpled

Kate Blewett and Brian Woods found this child confined to a chair in an orphanage in China. Their film, *The Dying Rooms*, shocked the world.

Photo: Kate Blewett/Brian Woods

bedclothes and drew back the covers. A baby girl about eighteen months old lay there, fighting for breath, her eyes covered in mucous, her lips parched, her skin stretched tautly over her emaciated skeleton. She clearly had only hours or a few days to live. The staff told us that the girl had fallen ill, but as they had no medicines, they had simply put her in this room and closed the door. That was ten days ago. For ten days, she had lain alone in the dark, starving to death.

We asked her name and were told Mei Ming. This means 'No Name'. Four days after we took her picture, Mei Ming lost her fight for life. She died of neglect. Her parents had abandoned her, and when we telephoned the orphanage, they denied she had ever existed. The only memory of her now is our film.

Titled *The Dying Rooms*, Brian and Kate's harrowing documentary made devastating television viewing but also demonstrated the impact that television could make.

I felt privileged when Brian and Kate interviewed me for the follow-up, *Return to the Dying Rooms*, screened in January 1996. We were aware that it would create waves initially for groups within the country but it was an important issue and I was determined to stand with this dedicated group of film makers.

The film featured Dr Zhang Shuyun, who had worked at the Shanghai Children's Welfare Institute, which had once been promoted by the Chinese government as a model of orphanages around the country. Dr Zhang had escaped with documents and photographs showing evidence of official indifference and brutality. She revealed that the majority of deaths that occurred from 1988 to 1993 were the deliberate result of 'summary resolution'. The purpose of the policy was to limit the number of children in order to maintain the workload at a constant level. When a new orphan or group of orphans arrived, child-care workers would agree amongst themselves to eliminate an equal number of the children already living on the ward, thereby holding the population constant. Once selected, the children would be denied virtually all food and medical care, and sometimes water. These children would simply become listless and fade away.

Di Wiang, a disabled twelve-year old boy, was a victim of 'summary resolution'. In *Death by Default*, published by Human Rights Watch, Dr Zhang explained:

> In February 1992, shortly after being targeted for 'summary resolution', Di attempted to steal food from other children, and was then drugged with chlorpromazine by the staff and tied down to his bed. During a visit to the orphanage by a group of foreigners later that month, Di was briefly untied and managed to escape to a bathroom on the ward, where he drank urine from the toilet … Di Wiang died from third degree malnutrition on February 23, 1992.

The Chinese authorities responded swiftly to Brian and Kate's documentary. The orphanages were traced and the directors summoned to Beijing. In an extraordinary move, virtually unprecedented, the Chinese Embassy in London issued a press release denouncing the film as 'a mean-spirited deceitful fabrication'. The statement, entitled '*The Dying Rooms* turns out to be fake', asserted that the British film crew misrepresented a storeroom as a room where children had been left to die, and blamed Kate for the death of Mei Ming. The film, the Chinese said, was 'full of vicious fabrications and contemptible lies.'

Brian and Kate's films would eventually be seen by one hundred million people in thirty-seven countries. No one could watch it and remain unmoved and it forced people to get involved – by giving money, campaigning or adopting an orphan.

We worked closely with Brian and Kate, lobbying the authorities to improve the care of orphans. In time, things got a little better as the authorities acknowledged the need for better standards and foreigners were allowed to assist in some orphanages.

The Killing Fields of Burma

The situation inside the killing fields of Burma was hidden from the world for many years. The people of Burma live under a military regime that has deliberately targeted its ethnic minorities, such as the Karen, for systematic genocide. It has regularly forced people to flee their homes as well as routinely practising torture, rape and other human rights abuses. Although democratic elections were held in 1990, when the National League for Democracy won a landslide victory, the Burmese ruling junta refused to recognise the result. Burma is a former British colony which gained its independence in 1948.

In 1991 we hosted the government-in-exile for Parliamentary meetings, but little happened till David Alton undertook a clandestine mission into Burma in 1998. He was visibly moved by the experience and wrote this powerful article on his return

> The military have transformed the once peaceful land of Burma into a vast concentration camp, where genocide and ethnic cleansing as ruthless as Bosnia occur on a daily basis.
>
> Burma's regime is deliberately targeting the Karen and other minorities. Driven from their homes and shot on sight, many have fled into the jungles or taken refuge in

camps in Thailand. But they are still not safe. Just weeks after I visited one camp, it was attacked and tragically, one pregnant woman was killed outright. Since then, several have died from their injuries, including a fifteen-year old girl and a four-year old boy.

From all that I saw and heard I was left in no doubt that after fifty years of independence from Britain, Burma remains an oppressive authoritarian state. People told me devastating stories of torture and brutality. Four Karen women in Papum were raped before suffering terrible deaths. Burmese soldiers stamped upon the stomachs of two pregnant women, first killing the unborn babies and then their mothers. Karen women have been spiked to death by soldiers pushing bamboo poles through their bodies.

One American missionary told me, 'Desolation is everywhere. I saw abandoned rice fields, empty villages,

A young mother with her children inside Burma.
Photo: Karen Human Rights Group

destroyed homes. Field upon empty field. The land was desolate. Not even the birds sing.'

Britain needs to examine its conscience about the role which it played in the genesis of this tragedy and urgently challenge the repatriation of refugees to a country where torture, rape, slavery and death await them.

It is inconceivable that huge foreign investments should continue to be made in a country where the abuse of human rights is a daily pastime.

Eco-tourism ventures, the Ye-Tavoy railway, the Yadana pipeline – operated by the French company Total, and the US based Unocal – are just some infrastructure projects which have involved the use of forced labour, including children and pregnant women. The use of forced labour to build Burma's new roads, railways and hotels was a chill-ing historical re-run of the suffering of British prisoners of war at the hands of the Japanese on the Burma Railway.

Britain, under the last government, was one of Burma's biggest trading partners but the present Labour govern-ment has signalled its distaste for such investments.

Nobel Peace Laureate Aung San Suu Kyi and her party, the National League for Democracy, won a landslide victo-ry in 1990 with 80% of the parliamentary seats, but the gen-erals placed her under house arrest and cracked down on the party.

Britain promised the Karen people an independent state but nothing was done. The Karen National Liberation Army have been fighting for autonomy since 1949 in what has been called the world's longest-running civil war. General Saw Bo Mya served in the KNLA, after his demob from Britain's Force 136, which bravely and valiantly resisted the Japanese during World War II. The General told me he blamed the British for the Karen's plight. He said, 'We are the allies you have abandoned and forgotten.'

Inside Burma's jungles, a catastrophe is waiting to happen in a country with ethnic cleansing every bit as ruthless as Bosnia and genocide every bit as cruel as Rwanda. Atrocities in Bosnia shocked European sensibilities only because courageous reporters ensured that the story was told. Politicians reacted with international and judicial sanctions while trials for war crimes have been established in the Hague.

Compare that with our reaction to Burma. What is intolerable in Europe should not be tolerated in South East Asia.

Is a life in South East Asia worth less than a life in South East Europe?

David was relentless in bringing this neglected issue to the world's attention while our campaign challenged companies such as Total and Britain's Premier Oil to pull out, as there was overwhelming evidence that foreign investment propped up the military regime.

Meanwhile, we helped Pastor Timothy Laklem to set up a fish farm to feed an entire community but in April 2000, the Burmese military attacked the camp and everything was destroyed. Despite this, we continued to send food and supplies through trusted contacts who risked their lives to take practical help to displaced Karen families hiding in the jungle.

When James Mawdsley was sentenced to eighteen years in jail for holding a peaceful protest inside the country, Jubilee Campaign led the battle for his release. We welcomed his zeal and enthusiasm and were relieved when he decided, following his release, that his future activism would be conducted from long range.

While foreign companies such as Total keep the generals in business and innocent families are hunted down, our campaign remains resolute to seek real change in Burma. We have no option.

Poison Gas Attack

In 1988, Saddam Hussein singled out the small town of Halabja for attack, because the local Kurdish population had sided with Iran in the eight-year war with Iraq.

A helicopter flew low over the town, just eleven kilometres from the Iranian border, but no one paid it much attention. Besides, the townspeople had grown accustomed to shoot-outs and gunfire.

But this was different. Over three days, starting at 6.20pm on 16 March, wave after wave of bombers attacked the town of eighty thousand people. Soon after the conventional bombing, planes dropped a lethal cocktail of poison gas: mustard gas, the nerve agents sarin, tabun, and allegedly VX, the most lethal of all.

There was a smell of garlic and apples as clouds of gas hung over the town and the surrounding hills, blotting out the sky. The chemicals soaked into people's clothes, skin, eyes, and lungs.

Five thousand died within hours. Entire families perished as they sought shelter in their own homes. Thousands who tried to flee the town were trapped, their escape route blocked by clouds of deadly gases that had contaminated everything in their path. Others flung themselves into a pond to wash off the chemicals but died within minutes.

Halabja entered the history books as the largest chemical weapon attack ever launched against a civilian population in modern times.

Investigative film maker, Gwynne Roberts, alerted the world to the massacre and his award-winning film, *The Winds of Death*, carried haunting, unforgettable images: women and children struck down in the streets; cars filled with bodies; a father who tried to shield his twins from the poisonous gas.

The poison gas attack brought some international condemnation, but at the time, Saddam Hussein was essential to the Middle Eastern foreign policy of the world's most powerful nation. Iraq had been given tacit support by the west in its war with Iran, in which one and a half million people perished. Time passed and Halabja was quietly forgotten by the world.

Ten years later, Gwynne Roberts was smuggled back into Halabja. This time he took Professor Christine Gosden, a leading British geneticist, with him. It was a dangerous mission and they had armed guards during their trip.

After examining hundreds of local people, the team recorded evidence of long-term irreversible genetic damage and discovered that the devastating legacy of the chemical attack lived on in the survivors a decade later.

Cancers were unusually aggressive, some extremely rare, and numbers had multiplied alarmingly amongst

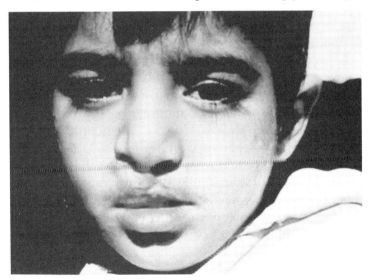

A Kurdish child in Halabja.
Photo: Gwynne Roberts

children. Miscarriages and infertility in couples had increased significantly. Professor Gosden examined a foetus in the hospital and found that the unborn child had injuries consistent with chemical weapons poisoning. She was told that no one had recently given birth to a normal baby. Leukaemia, Down's syndrome, lung disorders and heart diseases had all doubled, trebled or quadrupled in the town, while deformities such as harelips and cleft palates had increased amongst new born babies.

Gwynne Roberts' new television documentary, *Saddam's Secret Time Bomb*, exposed a chilling scene. The landscape was apocalyptic, the people desolate. Courageous doctors did what they could in pitiful conditions, in a hospital that was barren. Needles were recycled, disinfectants and basic anaesthetics non-existent. The local orphanage had no stove or cooking facilities and only one dismal room to shelter the children.

Gwynne's film showed that Saddam Hussein, now demonised by the west, had been supplied with chemical ingredients by the same western countries that backed military strikes against Iraq. Rolf Ekeus, former head of the United Nations inspectorate, charged with destroying Iraq's weapons of mass destruction, conceded that a secret deal to conceal the identity of the suppliers had been approved by the UN Security Council. He told the film makers, 'I think the decision I took, together of course with the International Atomic Energy Agency, was that for the time being, during investigation, we will protect the names for the purpose of getting information.' Ekeus, who went on to become Sweden's ambassador to the United States, said governments would 'never have forgiven us' if the UN weapons inspectors had disclosed the identities of supplier companies.

As a small charity, I assumed that there was little we could do, given the enormity of the problem, but Gwynne told us that virtually no aid had reached Halabja and things were desperate. 'Anything you can do, no matter how small, would be useful,' Gwynne told me.

I rang Ron George, of World in Need, who had worked with OM in Iran in 1963 and remained involved with the Kurds, the world's most numerous stateless people. Ron already knew of a local church network in the country who would help but said, 'It's dangerous. Saddam has a bounty on the head of anyone going into Kurdistan.'

With Ron's help, we delivered supplies and equipment to the hospital and a fresh water well was drilled at the School for Orphans, bringing uncontaminated water to the centre for the first time. As support became available, we sent it in.

Halabja's people found it ironic that Saddam Hussein's regime had now been condemned as forming part of an 'axis of evil'. In the not too distant past, the west provided tacit support for the dictator and almost no one had attempted to investigate or comprehend the epic scale of the disaster or to provide help for the survivors. With threats of a biological or chemical attack on the west by Saddam or Osama bin Laden's Al Qaeda network, one day our political leaders may wish they had paid Halabja more attention.

A recent visitor to Halabja told me that people didn't want to move from their homes in Halabja. All around were remnants from the attack, though the fields were fertile and the local shops sell produce from soil that was never thoroughly tested. Some stone houses were still in ruins, while the graveyards were marked by jagged rocks now overrun by fields of wheat and barley.

The one obvious sign of the tragedy was a simple memorial on the main road. Two figures in stone, of a man in a last futile attempt to shield his grandson.

13

You Can Run but You Can't Hide

Shay phoned me from Manila. 'It's tough going,' he said. He was sweating, after several hours going through dusty files in rusty filing cabinets at police headquarters. Shay was on the look-out for evidence of British men who had been arrested for child sex offences. We needed this information for a report that we were producing to launch our campaign in 1992 to fight child prostitution.

We knew the scam. If anyone was caught, they paid a small fine, wriggled out of the police handcuffs, burnt their passport, reported it lost, picked up temporary papers from the Embassy till they could get another passport, and were then free to continue their abuse elsewhere. When they returned home, their secret was safe. But paedophile behaviour wasn't triggered by geography. If they offended overseas, they would offend at home.

Before leaving, they would pay a few pesos to get their rap sheet removed from the police file. If a justice-driven detective like Shay were on their trail, all they would find was the empty brown folder.

But Shay was wily, had contacts, and his own files rivalled those of the authorities. We had decided to publish a list of names of such offenders in a documented report on child prostitution compiled from Shay's files.

It would be launched at a meeting we would organise in the House of Commons to call for a change in the law. As secretariat to the All Party Parliamentary Group on Street Children (APPGSC) we arranged for the group to host the meeting.

While editing the 162-page report, I went over the list of offenders and noticed that some Europeans on the list had schools listed as their addresses and one, in the UK, had a phone number. On impulse, I dialled the number, and to my astonishment the person answered the name I called out. We were both equally startled, as he demanded to know how I had obtained his number, and I was astounded at the accuracy of the information that Shay had uncovered.

A few days before the meeting in Parliament, I woke up in a sweat. What if the people on the list sued us for reprinting their details? I telephoned Shay immediately, and sounded the alarm.

Wilfred Wong and David Alton present our report on child prostitution to His Holiness Pope John Paul II.

Photo: Vatican Press

'We could end up in court,' I said, clearly panicked.

'Great,' Shay thundered, down a crackly line from the Philippines. 'Can you imagine the scene? You're in court and the paedophile offender is suing you for exposing him?'

'But he could file a suit against us,' I countered.

'Don't worry if you get sued, I'll raise the money for your bail!' Shay chuckled down the phone.

Shay calmed me down. 'Keep your nerve,' he counselled. It was a dangerous strategy but the right one. The risk was worth taking.

Copies of the report were sent to Scotland Yard, MPs and the media who attended our meeting in Parliament.

We were the first to call for a change in the law in 1992 to prosecute British sex tourists who abused children overseas. We wanted child prostitution outlawed, declared a crime against humanity. At this time, no foreign government or western nation had ever arrested any of its citizens who had abused children overseas and there was simply no mechanism in place to prosecute such offenders. Later other governments were to introduce such legislation, leaving Britain lagging behind.

The statistics proved sobering. Every year, about one million children were lured or forced into prostitution. This figure was documented in a Norwegian government report, confirming that young children were held as bait for a thriving attraction: sex with children.

Globally, as many as ten million children were thought to be enslaved in the sex industry, prostitution and pornography. Child prostitution tended to be higher in Asia and Latin America, although an alarming growth rate had been recorded in Africa, North America and Europe. Eastern Europe and the former communist states had emerged as a new market in the sexual exploitation of children.

The UN Rapporteur on Child Trafficking had remarked recently that the children being tricked into prostitution were getting younger and younger. 'These are nine, ten, eleven, twelve year old kids,' he said. The experts warned that the trend would increase unless action was taken.

Shay combined eloquence with clarity as he presented the historical context from which to view this crime, 'Sex tourism and child prostitution is the ultimate in exploitation. Peoples of other nations have exploited the raw materials of poorer countries for centuries. Now they're coming back to exploit the bodies of our children.'

Our campaign emphasised that the authorities that should have brought men such as Andrew Harvey to justice had failed, and they had used the system to evade capture, thus putting more children at risk. It was time to cry 'Enough!' Action was needed. The law must be changed.

It's easy to launch a project with flashy publicity material and sound bites but it's imperative to maintain the pressure. The government's initial response wasn't encouraging.

At a meeting led by MPs from the APPGSC, the Home Office told us that it was too complex a problem and the law couldn't be changed to accommodate our demands. It would never happen. Their logic was that such laws would be unworkable in practice because of the difficulties they perceived in gathering sufficient evidence from foreign jurisdictions to facilitate a successful prosecution. This argument was advanced despite the fact that similar laws existed for offences such as murder, suggesting that they would accept evidence for this, but not for crimes against children. The Home Office insisted that it was not for the British government to impose its laws abroad. That was that. To strengthen our efforts we joined ECPAT (End Child Prostitution and Asian Tourism) but continued several independent initiatives on the issue.

In 1994, our Parliamentary Officer, Wilfred Wong, a barrister-at-law, drafted a Bill setting out in detail the laws we sought. Wilfred put a requirement of Double Criminality in the Bill. This meant that the alleged child sex offence had to be considered as a criminal offence both in the foreign land where it occurred and within the UK before the accused could be charged and prosecuted in this country. He explained

> I did this because there was no way the British government would agree to imposing its laws on another jurisdiction if the crime in question was not even considered an offence in that foreign jurisdiction.
>
> Furthermore, I put in the requirement that nothing in the bill would contravene the legal principle of Double Jeopardy. This meant that if the defendant had already been prosecuted and either convicted or acquitted for the offence while abroad, he could not be prosecuted for the same offence again when he returned to Britain.

At the time, Parliament was considering the Criminal Justice Bill and ECPAT persuaded Lord Archer of Sandwell, QC, a former Solicitor General in the Labour government, to table our Bill as an amendment to the Criminal Justice Bill. Conservative government opposition ensured its failure but Lord Hylton, the independent crossbench peer, picked it up again in the House of Lords.

On the day before its second reading in Parliament, Glenda Jackson MP delivered Jubilee's twenty thousand-strong petition to Downing Street and captured considerable television and radio coverage in its support. Hours later, the government let it be known that it would oppose the passage of Hylton's Bill in the Commons. Their compromise was to consider prosecuting sex tour operators instead. Clearly someone had watched the ITV report. In Parliamentary code, this was the Bill's death knell, but no one was surprised. The government continued to argue that the Bill was unworkable and predictable form letters sped off Whitehall's word processors to anyone who inquired. However, that argument was decisively squashed, in June 1995, when a Swedish court successfully prosecuted a sixty-nine year old former civil servant, Bengt Bolin, for sexual intercourse with a fourteen year old boy while on holiday in Thailand on 18 February 1993.

The British government was put under further pressure with the increasing media coverage.

In 1995, Glenda Jackson and Aninha Capaldi took our protest to the door of Downing Street.

*   *   *   *

The *News of the World* hit the streets with a bang. Roger's investigation was splashed across the front page.

Roger had done well. Although sensational in style (what could we expect, this was the *News of the World*, after all), I thought it was restrained in its detail.

And there they were in the newspaper, Clarke, Teasdale, Fitzgerald.

With nearly five million people buying copies of the *News of the World* all across the country, Britain's top-selling newspaper guaranteed that people everywhere were talking about the child sex industry. The question on everyone's lips was: why doesn't the government do something about this scandal?

It was the question we wanted answered. It was the question that we wouldn't allow to be buried.

A television documentary, called *Defender of the Children*, about Shay's work was screened nationwide in October 1995, and we previewed the hour-long programme for MPs and supporters in the House of Commons.

A reporter in the film asked UK officials why they hadn't followed the FBI's example of investigating suspected offenders that had been exposed. The pathetic response was, 'The FBI asked for their addresses.' The implication was that the US had actively followed up suspects but British officials had not. They hadn't even asked for addresses of offenders.

The reply caused spontaneous uproar at the Parliamentary meeting. Nigel Griffiths MP turned to me and said, 'If I was the Home Secretary, I would have been furious. I would have picked up the phone and expected a response on my desk the following morning.'

I could understand Nigel's outrage. He was the MP, with David Alton, who had chaired our first meeting in

Parliament in 1992, three years earlier, when we named Britons arrested in the report we published when our campaign was launched. This was the very same list that we had passed on to Scotland Yard, followed up by the TV reporter.

The Front Page

The media backed our campaign and Shay, Wilfred and I were regularly featured in a series of high profile news reports on television, radio and in the newspapers. But there was still unfinished business, with 747 Travel operating freely.

Had Michael Stone and Peter Mitchell been following the passage of this campaign through the media? Were they trembling with fear of being exposed or were they laughing because they had got away with it and were continuing to do so?

After one television interview, two reporters from the *Sunday Mirror* contacted our office with the question: 'Is there an investigation you're working on at the moment? Do you have any leads?'

It was time.

I handed the journalists the file marked 747 Travel and finally closed the door on ITV covering the story. The reporters offered money.

'I don't want any money,' I replied. 'I just want this story told.'

While some tabloid journalists seemed to enjoy a lurid reputation, in our dealings the Fleet Street press were professional and ethical.

I followed the story from afar and on Sunday, 31 December, awoke at 6am to buy the papers. Staring back at me were photos of Peter Mitchell and Michael Stone. The reporters had done their job. They asked the questions. And Mitchell and Stone went for it. Boastful, Mitchell was extensively quoted in the *Sunday Mirror* referring to child sex and encouraging the journalists to indulge themselves.

The *Sunday Mirror* had nailed them and I was pleased. If there was any doubt that the campaign to change the law was desperately needed, the newspaper had confirmed it with this investigation.

There was no turning back.

*   *   *   *

While the media maintained its public pressure, the government were also monitoring events unfolding behind the scenes in Ireland.

At his request, I flew over to join Father Shay at a high profile launch of the campaign in Dublin and our lobbying materials and reports were widely used.

Owen Ryan, an active TD (an Irish MP) heard one of the interviews and arranged an immediate meeting. Mr Ryan told us that he had drafted a Bill as early as June 1995 but as a member of the Opposition Fianna Fail Party, he didn't want it to become a victim of political intrigue.

'Child prostitution is a new form of slavery. It's outrageous that Irish citizens can be guilty of abusing children but escape punishment,' he insisted.

Strategic manoeuvres followed. Ironically, in London, one of Jubilee's supporters, Patricia Toomey, had been invited to the opening of the Irish Centre in Hammersmith to meet the special guest, Ireland's Deputy Prime Minister, Dick Spring. Not wanting to waste an opportunity, Patricia placed Jubilee Campaign's report in Mr Spring's hand. 'We need your help to change the law,' she told him. Mr Spring assured her that he would read the report and seriously consider what she had said.

Five days later, Ireland's Minister of Justice, Nora Owens, telephoned Father Shay at home in Dublin and told him, 'We would welcome the Bill even though it was from the Opposition.'

At 7pm on Tuesday, 14 November, the Bill was tabled in the Oireachtas (Irish Parliament) and Ireland joined America, Australia, Germany, Sweden, New Zealand, Belgium, France, Norway and Denmark in endorsing legislation that was now sweeping the tourist-sending countries.

One TV journalist from Ireland's main channel, RTE, told me that perhaps the most extraordinary factor was that the ruling government had accepted a Private Member's Bill from the Party in opposition – only the fourth in the history of the State. Sensibly, the contest for political supremacy was shelved and old adversaries united in the war against child prostitution.

The Irish Bill was introduced amidst predictable political manoeuvres, strategic media coverage and effective lobbying. It was a moment for activists to savour, a personal triumph for Father Shay, and demonstrative proof that campaigning works.

It was Ireland 1, Britain 0.

The Daniel Handley Murder

Brett Tyler was abandoned as a baby, raised in Barnardo's Homes, sexually assaulted at four, and met his first 'real' friend in prison, Timothy Morss, who had also been abused as a child. Both were serving time for sexual offences and became accomplices and lovers. In a special annexe of Wormwood Scrubs prison, the group therapy session for sex offenders heard the men discuss their ultimate fantasy, the final taboo. It was to abduct a young blond boy, abuse and murder him.

When they left prison, Tyler flew to the Philippines to pursue his obsession with little boys. Meanwhile Morss became the lover of another former inmate, David Guttridge and moved to Bradley Stoke, near Bristol, where they bought a house together. They also set up a minicab firm, Guy's Cars, in Camberwell, South London.

When Tyler returned to Britain in April 1994, he teamed up with Morss and revived their secret fantasy.

In October, the men went cruising. In East London, they spotted a young boy trying to fix the chain on his silver BMX bike.

'We were just looking at the boys, the usual hobby,' Tyler would recollect later, in his first police interview. 'We saw a boy riding a bike. He took a side street so we turned round and went back. We pulled over, put a map in the back of the car, asked him to show us where we were and pushed him in.'

The boy was Daniel Handley. He was blond. He was nine years old.

From a deprived background, Daniel earned extra pocket money by collecting trolleys from the local Asda supermarket and helping people with their shopping. Daniel was allowed to ride his bicycle out on his own, as long as he was home by 6pm.

On Sunday, 22 October 1994, he was late.

Tyler and Morss took Daniel back to Camberwell and in the flat above the car hire firm they videotaped themselves abusing the child. Daniel was then driven along the M4 in Morss' Peugeot estate car, which pulled up in a lay-by close to junction 14. He was strangled with a knotted rope and buried in a shallow grave in woods adjoining Bradley Stoke, near the house that Morss shared with Guttridge. Two weeks later, Tyler and Morss returned to bury the body deeper in the ground. Both then took off for the Philippines. Tyler followed a similar pattern using a video camera to record his abuse with a dozen videotapes as evidence. In one tape, he is seen haggling over the price of sex and reducing it from the equivalent of 75p to 50p.

Tyler and Morss liked the Philippines because they could continue to abuse children and no one would know. They could get away with it. But eventually they fell out and Morss returned to the UK, where Daniel's disappearance had triggered a massive police hunt and intensive media coverage. Six months later, in March 1995, foxes disturbed Daniel's grave and a man walking his dog discovered the body.

In May, a BBC TV *Crimewatch* programme gave the hunt for the killers even more publicity and the programme triggered memories from a psychiatrist and prison officer from Wormwood Scrubs. They rang police the next day with the names of the wanted men.

But old-fashioned detective work had also paid off. As the police searched for links between East London and Bristol, they learned of the house in Bradley Stoke owned by Morss and Guttridge. Their names went straight to the top of the list of suspects.

Morss was arrested.

The net was closing on Tyler and his days on the run were at an end. The police were given a clue.

Olongapo City.

I was in the Philippines visiting Father Shay when the call came through. It was from Superintendent Kevin MacTavish, a senior policeman attached to the Australian Embassy in Manila. He told Shay that Scotland Yard had sought his advice in helping to trace the wanted man. MacTavish could think of only one person who could track down the fugitive – Shay – and gave him the name of the man Scotland Yard were hunting.

Brett Tyler.

'I'll get on the case straight away,' Shay told the Australian lawman.

He put an experienced investigator on the trail and they located Tyler's hideout. At the time, some children were thought to be in the house. Tyler had won over the locals by paying for a few kids' school fees. Tyler also posed as a priest and held church services in an outhouse. Shay asked for the fullest details of Tyler's house with possible escape routes and the information was passed down the line. Based on Shay's documentation, two Scotland Yard detectives flew out within days and Tyler was arrested for immigration violations and deported for overstaying his visa. This was considered the only way to capture the sex killer.

Tyler left behind incriminating photographs and letters. In one note, he wrote 'Kill the children for me.'

One year later, as the case came to trial, prosecutor John Bevan told the jury, 'You will hear evidence about as depressing an example of the dark side of human nature, man's inhumanity to man and downright wickedness as you can imagine.'

The tragic story of Daniel Handley caused a sensation. Like everyone else, we were gripped by the distressing case. It provided the most dramatic example yet of how sex tourists could travel with impunity and the ease with which they could conceal their movements. Even when arrested, Tyler had to be chased from the Philippines on an immigration offence. More importantly, Tyler had abused children in Britain and the Philippines but he was hunted for the crime that he had committed in London. His crimes in Olongapo City were ignored and went unpunished. This disturbing signal told men they could continue to travel abroad, abuse children, and get away with it.

The increasing media coverage, followed by the Irish Bill, and now the Daniel Handley case, had finally hit home. That year, the government did a sudden U-turn and announced that they would introduce extra-territorial laws for sex offences against children and would incorporate this into the 1997 Sex Offenders Act. Much of the legislation was modelled on the Bill that Jubilee Campaign's Parliamentary Officer, Wilfred Wong, had drafted two years earlier.

The government also introduced a sex register for offenders. The Home Office intended to impose a three months' penalty for not registering but Wilfred recommended that this should be upgraded and consequently this was increased to six months' imprisonment and a stiffer fine.

When news broke about the change in the law, many of our supporters – and some journalists – called to share in our celebration. It was an important, even historic, campaign.

I was surprised that it had taken so long, and had been such a struggle, to convince the authorities. What could be more important than protecting our children?

High profile cases, such as those of Sarah Payne and Amanda Dowler, confirm that abductions and sex crimes against children require further resources for the police and mechanisms for swift action. Crimes against children should be given equal priority as murder and terrorism.

Anyone who harms a child should get this message: You can run but you can't hide.

14

Rescue the Children

Bombay was humid and muggy and I was glad I was only staying twenty-four hours. A 'high tech' metropolis with real estate that matched New York in price, several blue chip companies had moved their back room operation here. I'd spent several months in Bombay as a youth with Operation Mobilisation but didn't think the city had anything special to reveal.

I'd hastily rearranged flights after I'd been urged to visit a local worker. Just an hour after I landed on a sultry evening in February 1996, Reverend K.K. Deveraj led me into the nadir of Bombay's notorious red light district, a voyage that was only possible because he'd won the trust of people inside the network.

Deveraj had spent over three years helping boys hooked on drugs and consequently learned that their sisters and mothers were enslaved prostitutes. This contact gave him unprecedented access amongst the girls and women who patrolled the back streets and alleys of Kamathipura. Many children from the area wanted to get away but he had nowhere to take them.

Remarkably, several of the children had developed a strong personal faith and attended church services he held nearby. Some of the prostitutes wandered into the meeting and for that hour, business in the red light district slowed down. For a few minutes, the girls could lose themselves in songs of praise and prayers of hope. Amidst such humiliation and shame, the women responded to this message of deliverance.

By the time we reached Kamathipura, light was fading. I could tell we were close, as girls with heavy make-up in brightly coloured saris lined the street corners in a silent parade.

Fourteenth Lane snaked its way about one hundred yards down, a muddy road with narrow houses on the left, mud huts and makeshift shelters on the right. Ramshackle wooden buildings, each a different colour. Hands and elbows leaned on window ledges. Faces peered down. On the street, girls with painted faces, brightly coloured bangles that jingle, jangled. The eyes winked enticingly, but seemed strangely dead.

Deveraj estimated that about three thousand girls lived on Fourteenth Lane and that the Kamathipura area was home to about twenty thousand prostitutes, now called 'commercial sex workers'. Bombay, with a population of about thirteen million, was said to have over one hundred thousand prostitutes.

The women in the area trusted him and so I learned some of their stories. Sharlinka wasn't sure how old she was. She was enticed from Andhra Pradesh with the offer of a job but was sold to a brothel-owner. She'd been held captive for about five years but wasn't sure.

'I had to work hard,' she told us. 'The men were fat, old and smelly. I was forced to do some disgusting things. I wasn't allowed out for three years.'

Another young girl with sad eyes said, 'I'm from Calcutta. I don't have any relatives, only a mother, but I'm not sure where she is now. I drifted around and ended up in Bombay. I was caught one night by several men, they told me they'd find work for me and I'd have a good life but I was sold into slavery.'

She had graceful features but a dejected expression. When asked her age she speculated, 'I'm about fourteen or fifteen, maybe even sixteen, but I don't really know.' This girl said she didn't want to go back to the brothel and looked worried. 'I don't have anyone in this world who cares for me. No one knows whether I live or die.'

As she listened intently to Deveraj's words of solace, her eyes widened in silent wonder. It's as though she'd heard about some extraordinary discovery or the plot of an intriguing film. She hung on Deveraj's every word. Tears formed in her eyes. She bit her fingernails.

There were several Nepali girls with pale olive skin, soft features and long angular bodies. Girls were trafficked from Nepal by underworld gangs with police connivance. They were held in a slave market and brothel-owners visited the auction to buy the girls. From Bombay, some of the girls – and boys – were dispatched to Goa, now India's most popular tourist resort.

The girls sold to the brothels worked to pay off their debt. Customers paid the brothel and the girls survived on tips. This system of debt bondage kept them in virtual slavery. The girls were held in appalling circumstances, beaten and abused, with little opportunity of ever being liberated from this vicious circle of servitude. In many cases, the girls had no idea when their debt would be paid off – if ever – and were resigned to a life of enslavement. Girls charged between Rs 50 (£1) and Rs 250 (£5) and yes, everything was available with no limits to these sexual encounters.

Bombay's red light district had a heavy gang influence and there were many stories of shoot-outs and stabbings.

Suicides were spoken of factually. Very few got away. Anyone caught trying to escape was beaten severely when they returned. One girl, Mina, tried to jump out of a top floor window but fell and broke her back. She had been caged for seven years and forbidden to leave her room. Usually the girls are kept for two to three years before they're allowed out on their own.

AIDS is a time bomb waiting to happen, an explosion predicted by statisticians destined to turn India into one of the major crisis capitals of the world. Predictably, it wasn't hard to find statistics: twenty per cent of Bombay's commercial sex workers were under eighteen and up to fifty per cent of these children are thought to be HIV positive.

To the girls themselves AIDS wasn't such a threat. They have problems staying alive. Surviving tonight. Tomorrow was twenty-four hours away.

Night had fallen and the back streets of Bombay were full of girls. A narrow space between the buildings revealed an alley, an active corridor leading deeper into the quicksand. A furtive glance into the warren exposed more verandahs, more bright saris, more girls. Somewhere from the midst of the labyrinth, a baby cried, an old man sat crumpled, staring into the distance. Life went on.

Deveraj told me there was a girl he wanted me to meet and we tramped back and forth through the alleys and dark, narrow passageways on a mission to locate her. It was late at night but the streets were crowded and dirty. A woman scavenged through rubbish that was piled up at least fifteen foot high, sprawling everywhere. A child ran across and kicked the garbage playfully. No one stared, no one was surprised.

After twenty minutes, we learn that the girl we were pursuing was at a nearby school where floor space was provided for a few destitute children to sleep. 'She's safe for a few more hours,' Deveraj sighed. 'I don't like her being in this area at night. It's just not safe. Anything can happen.'

The school had locked their gates because of the lateness of the hour but she was summoned and within minutes an elegant, slender and strikingly beautiful young girl appeared behind the bars of the gate. She talked for a while, while I stayed back in the shadows, observing the scene.

In the dim hallway, a coloured light from a nearby neon sign shone on her.

It was hard to define, an inexplicable timeless moment, stirred by an unusual sense of the presence of God. I didn't know her name but felt my heart aflame and planted like a seed within me, an affection between a father and a daughter. Here amidst the rubbish, squalor, corruption and oppression, the painted faces, the very presence of a slave kingdom, the overwhelming sense of desolation, she glowed like a precious jewel. I wanted to capture the spirit of this defining moment and the scene around us but it was too dangerous to sneak a photograph. As we retraced our steps and walked back to the car, I heard her story.

Asha's mother was a prostitute who had lived on Fourteenth Lane, just around the corner from us, the street of shame that we'd just walked down. Asha grew up in a cramped squalid room, virtually a cage, where her mother serviced between ten and twenty-five customers a day. Most of the time, Asha and her younger sister and brother were forced to loiter in the street, but many nights she fell asleep, curled up in a corner of the room, waiting for the last customer to leave.

When her mother died, there was almost no time for tears. The brothel-owners moved a young Nepali girl into the cage, and Asha and her younger siblings were dumped in the street outside the brothel where her

mother had worked. A makeshift canvas hut granted
sanctuary from the scorching summer heat and the driving monsoon rain.

The young urchin family ate leftovers given them by
friendly prostitutes, scrounged scraps from the rubbish
dump, and begged for paisa from passing trade. Their
survival was a remarkable record of resilience amidst
grinding despair and degradation.

The brothel owners kept a custodial eye on Asha and
her sister, as, inevitably, the children of prostitutes always
followed their parents into the sex industry. The word on
the street was that Asha's mother's boyfriend, a taxi
driver, lied and said that he was her father, and was negotiating a deal with one of the brothel owners, expecting
about £600 for the sale of this beautiful young girl. That
was a small fortune, equivalent to several years' salary,
for him. It was money he just couldn't refuse.

Asha at fourteen when I met her in Bombay.
Photo: Danny Smith

The turning point in her life came when she met Deveraj and told him that she wanted to escape. His reply was, 'Have faith. With God everything is possible.' But with each passing day the tension was mounting. She was repulsed by the sexual remarks from local men but there was no escape, nowhere to hide. Every time she spotted the chubby church worker, she chased after him and tugged at his sleeve. 'Uncle! Uncle!' she called out. 'When will you take me away?'

Asha wanted to turn her back on the past. She wanted to wave goodbye to Fourteenth Lane for ever. She told him, 'I want to leave. I feel dirty here. I'll never forget this street but all the memories are bad. I don't like the way the men look at me. Some men want me to join them. They say they'll look after my brother and sister. I sense the danger. Every day it's getting harder for me to live here. I know I can't fight them for ever. It's a question of time. I want to leave here but I have nowhere to go. No one wants me except the brothel owners.'

The next day, Deveraj had arranged for some of the girls, including Asha, to meet me at his office and I was struck at just how young and fragile the children seemed. They were dressed smartly with their hair done and one by one they lined up against the wall and I took a portrait photograph of each of them. Asha, the oldest of the children, was last. She faced the camera. Her eyes were alive with the half glint of a smile. The awkwardness of the meeting, the formality of the soundings and the stilted conversation conveyed little of their circumstances.

It was time to leave Bombay and as Deveraj drove me to the airport, I asked what would become of Asha.

'The daughters of prostitutes have all followed their mothers into the sex business,' Deveraj said. 'Very few get away alive.'

'But could she be rescued?' It was the question that I carried with me.

Deveraj felt that the only way to make a difference was to establish a residential home outside the city where orphaned and abandoned children of prostitutes could find sanctuary. It seemed an insignificant gesture given the scale of the problem but if we couldn't rescue Asha, it was clear she would be condemned to a life sentence of sexual slavery.

On the flight back home, the image of Asha alone in the red light district haunted me. With it came the realisation that if we were unable to purchase a building, the doors of another house would open for Asha and her life would change for ever.

It was a question of time, a race that I was convinced we must win.

* * * *

A Home for Asha

Backstage politics created tension within the office circle, as there seemed an unwillingness to support the project. I took the materials home and, over the weekend, we bundled hundreds of letters that I personally signed with photographs from my trip, and mailed them out. Although the photograph of Asha wasn't 'dramatic', it seemed to have an anointing as many people were moved and responded generously.

This had become a personal mission and I treasured each response and every pound that came in. As with other projects, one hundred per cent of every donation went directly as designated and within a few months our prayers were answered – we hit our target. Deveraj

located land two hours outside of Bombay and personally designed a grand house that was built in record
time. Finally, we had a home for Asha.

Asha collected all her belongings into a cardboard box
and waited at the corner and when the car pulled up to
rescue her, she climbed in and never looked back at
Kamathipura's Fourteenth Lane. Five other girls came
with her, including her sister and also her brother.

The money came from various sources, mostly indi-
viduals with small, sacrificial gifts. One of the larger gifts
came from George and Olivia Harrison after it was
agreed that a portion of the sales from the Beatles'
Anthology project would be donated to charity. With
George and Olivia's gift, through the Apple Foundation,
we were able to pay the entire running costs for the
home for a year.

Sometime earlier, Steve Brown, Billy Connolly's man-
ager, called and asked if we needed money as they had
announced a benefit concert during Billy's five week
sell-out residency at Hammersmith's Apollo Theatre in
1997. I sent Steve three projects to choose from. Minutes
before Billy walked on stage, Steve told him about our
plans to build a home for orphaned and abandoned children of prostitutes and showed him Asha's photograph.
Billy walked on stage clutching her photo and for the first
few minutes of the show, talked movingly about Asha and
explained where the money from that night's performance
would be spent. He then delicately placed Asha's photograph on the stool beside him, commenced his act, and
within minutes had his audience in stitches. While three
thousand people in the theatre were crying with laughter,
almost falling out of their chairs, I sat riveted in my seat in
the tenth row with tears of joy rolling down my face. I
could see Asha's photograph in front of me. She seemed to
be looking directly at me. She was smiling.

Billy's concert produced a phenomenal amount of cash. We had the choice of playing it safe and keeping the money for several years running costs for the home, or we could build another home, so that even more children could be rescued.

Within a few months, a second, equally impressive home was built, again from Deveraj's original design, and over the next few years, more than seventy girls were rescued from Bombay's red light district. Each one told a heartrending story. If it wasn't for this extraordinary work, these girls would be condemned to a life of perpetual enslavement.

When I raised the difficulty of recurring operational costs for both homes with Steve, he came up with the brilliant idea of launching Tickety-Boo Tea, with all the profits used for the project. In October 1999, Billy Connolly invited the media and friends for a day on a tea clipper that sailed down the Thames to launch the innovative idea. Everyone who buys Tickety-Boo Tea contributes toward the running costs for the homes. Even I became a tea drinker.

It hasn't been easy for Asha. She was hospitalised for TB, struggled with her studies, found it hard to fit in with the others in the home, and experienced predictable teenage problems. Although cheerful and bright, she had a melancholic side, and one evening when I was in Bombay, she told me, 'I'm sad but I don't know why.'

Overcoming tremendous obstacles, she enrolled at one of Bombay's top colleges. But the students found out about her background and she had to endure their taunts. She was resilient and strong and faced her accusers head on – a challenge she eventually triumphed over.

In 2002, she married Sanjay, and Deveraj gave me the honour of giving Asha away – one of the most special days of my life. Sanjay worked with Deveraj's team and had known her for several years. The wedding was planned for 25 June but it was also the day that the newspapers predicted would have the heaviest rainfall of the monsoon season. Everyone prayed that the rains would be delayed by twenty-four hours and with extraordinary timing, the cloudburst came just hours after the reception ended.

Both Asha and Sanjay are now employed by Jubilee Action working with Deveraj's outreach programme for poor people in Bombay. Deveraj's vision has been inspiring and over time, we have developed a unique partnership with his organisation, Bombay Teen Challenge.

* * * *

The local municipality in the red light area were impressed with Deveraj's work and offered us premises to operate a night shelter for the children of prostitutes.

Asha's wedding in June 2002. A radiant bride on an unforgettable day.

The shelter was ideally located in the centre of Bombay's sex industry and would provide prostitutes' children with a safe haven at night, the moment of greatest risk. The children would be fed, get basic medical attention, Christian counselling, and encouragement to attend school. The shelter would give us a foothold right inside the sex trade and increase our team's influence in the area. It would enable us to keep a watchful eye on these children as they grew and help to prevent them from entering the sex business.

The property required refurbishment but before we released funds for the work to be completed, I asked Deveraj how we could be sure it would be used for those at greatest risk? The question was answered – like many others – with a telephone call.

'There's a baby for sale in one of the brothels. She's about to be sold,' the man said. 'Come quickly or it'll be too late.'

Our homes in Bombay care for orphaned and abandoned children of prostitutes. Over seventy girls have been rescued since the mission started.

Photo: Rev. K.K. Deveraj

Deveraj charged out of the office and raced to Kamathipura.

The nine month old girl's father worked as a street labourer, the poorest of the poor, in Bombay's bustling vegetable market. Tragedy struck when the child's mother died. In turmoil, unable to cope, and with intense financial pressures, the father took his daughter to Kamathipura, the centre of the sex industry.

The man toured the brothels and in a moment of madness, offered the baby for sale. The news caused a mini sensation as the brothel owners bargained over the innocent child. The man was offered £150.

The money was a significant amount for the labourer. Just as he was musing over the deal, Deveraj burst into the airless room located at the back of one of the brothels. After some discussion, Deveraj realised that the labourer was determined to sell the baby. Taking him

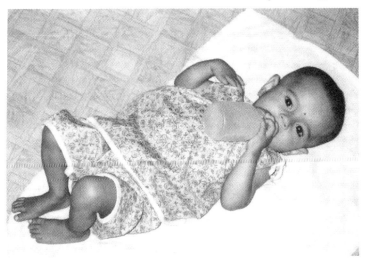

This is Glory. At nine months old she was offered for sale in Bombay's red light district.

Photo: Danny Smith

aside, Deveraj warned that there would be consequences and convinced him not to sell the child. The father eventually handed the girl into our care.

Deveraj accepted the child immediately. Any hesitation would have been catastrophic and the child would have been sold.

The rescue completed, the baby was safe. She was named Glory.

She was taken directly to our shelter, the first child to be given refuge, evidence of the need and the triumph that faith brings.

I was in Bombay as this remarkable story unfolded. I held Glory in my arms shortly after her deliverance and thanked God for the miraculous timing that enabled Deveraj to rescue this special child. It was wonderful that this millennium baby should be given freedom and a new life at the beginning of a new century.

14

What Tomorrow May Bring

Early Days

Jubilee Campaign's first office took over our living room and every available space in our home, with my Elvis memorabilia, *Rolling Stone* magazines and unpublished Dylan manuscript relegated to archive boxes in the garage and the loft.

The spin doctors would have classified us as on a 'mission impossible'. There was no marketing plan or fund-raising strategy, no publicity material – I was amused when George Verwer told me that it took Operation Mobilisation twenty years to come up with a mission statement – no office, no paid staff, all volunteers like me; no categorised list of assorted donors. The list was endless.

Jubilee was a gift and I felt my role was to be its custodian. I was determined that we should be broadly Christian, 'salt and light', positioned in the marketplace, with ninety-nine per cent of our time and money spent on our mission and one per cent spent on our administration. We sought an organic, natural growth but this simple approach caused continued tension as our passion exceeded our purse.

We live in an age of spin and sound bites, where publicity and hype exert undue influence and appear to dominate our world. It's easy to sell things to people and hard to know what's genuine and real any more. 'Package it right and they'll buy it. It's all about branding, you know.' With Jubilee Campaign, the compelling force was simply to find the best way to help people in need. The pressures were intense, matched only by the challenges. We didn't take on campaigns because there was money in the bank – there frequently wasn't. We did it because of the burning passion for justice that was a shared calling – and sometimes obsession – amongst the team. Every pound and every penny that people sent us was spent on the work and every time we launched a new campaign, we ran the risk of going bankrupt.

It's always emotional for me to retrace those early days. While I provided the strategic vision for the work, it was my family who made the sacrifice, and Joan who struggled with the financial burden of running a home with little money coming in. Joan's faithfulness, courage and dedication far exceeded my own. While my vision was both noble and global, I had obscured the very real needs of those nearest and dearest to me. I was MIA (missing in action) at home for lots of the time. I wasn't there and I didn't know it.

With the passing of time, I discovered that the important and real things in my life were the gifts that God had given me – my family. They had given meaning to my life and from this strengthened relationship has come a sense of belonging. I was finally at ease with myself.

Growing Up

Today things are so different. Jubilee has changed, almost beyond recognition, as we've taken huge strides towards becoming an efficient, professional organisation with a sustained focus on strengthening our foundations in order to help us grow. The revolution was complete with job descriptions, a business plan and a fund-raising strategy. I think my role is changing also. These days, I find that my mission is to inspire other people to have a mission.

In 2002, Dr Kim Tan, the chairman of Jubilee Action, introduced 'Business Partnerships', an innovative concept that will cause us to rethink how resources are used, in order to bring change for communities that are beyond the reach of traditional aid methods, and to transform the landscape of poverty. This brave new idea was launched at a reception at Downing Street to honour Jubilee Action's work, arranged through Aninha Capaldi's contact with the Prime Minister's wife, Cherie Blair. It was another landmark for Jubilee and an exciting moment in our development.

But who knows what tomorrow may bring? We live in extraordinary times with the drums of war and terrorism beating out a dangerous rhythm, with the smoke from the peace pipes obscured and distant. At Jubilee, we're determined not to get distracted, and to remember our commitment to those who aren't necessarily making front page news. We must remain resolute in our mission and vigilant in our work to protect and care for Children at Risk and the Suffering Church family worldwide. If we – and people like us – don't help, who will?

Personal Thanks

I can't believe this is down on paper.

Primary thanks are due to Ali Hull, who never gave up and created an original structure whereby this story could be told; and to Mark Finnie for his valuable contribution.

It's hard to write about current events, especially when you are a player in them. But my part was easy. Some moments left me scorched and are still hard to express in words. As a witness, I carry the responsibility, taking minimal comfort from the little victories on the journey, and, like many others, think of those streets we will never walk down, and those people we will never meet, who suffer in silence, and whose names are known only to the Lord. To seek to serve them is the challenge. And even as we bring our offering, we learn that we are the ones most in need, and who are rewarded by those we seek to help.

Frequently, I've felt like a spectator, both humbled and blessed by unfolding events, stimulated by dedicated people to work with, inspired by those who pulled alongside to lead, encourage and support.

With David Alton in the cockpit, a co-founder of Jubilee Campaign, the work was strengthened beyond anything we could have dreamt possible. His commitment never faltered from the first day we met and Jubilee Campaign's accomplishments within Parliament can be traced to his door.

Aninha proved a brilliant and beautiful ambassador, and Jim Capaldi an enthusiastic patron.

Dr Kim Tan found us recently but embraced us so fully.

The warriors of faith who raised their own support in those early days have a special place and many of the exploits in this book wouldn't have happened without them: Ann Buwalda, Richard Warnes, Howard Taylor, Rosie McLaughlin, Ali Kimber Bates, Robert Day, Stephen Andrews, John Anderson, Gerry Rogers.

The soldiers who followed made an important contribution. Thanks guys. Rachel Bader, Jennie Cain, Emily Murray, Lynda Ann Loring, Kate Baxendale, Kate Weeks, Alice Diamond, John Bolton, Alan Groves, Malcolm Grange, Kate Wyles, Arie de Pater. Wilfred Wong is a one-man action unit who never takes his eye off the target. Mark Rowland was recruited to run the campaign to free James Mawdsley from jail in Burma. When James was released, Mark stayed on and now leads the fund-raising offensive for Jubilee Action, with our excellent team: Kimseng Lim, Derek Williams, Lisa McKnight, Kumar Selvakumaran; David Osborne and Graham Brown; Ron Begbie. The steadfast, faithful and committed Ann Buwalda and her valiant crew – Bonnie Ryason, David Mundy, Tarik Radwan, Kie-Eng Go and not forgetting the Congressional Religious Liberty fellow, Karin Finkler on Capitol Hill – continue to storm the barricades.

There's something revitalising about the restoration of a relationship and that's how I felt when Mike Morris and I were back together again in 2002. His innovative plans for Jubilee Campaign are sure to have a strategic impact in the future. It's been so encouraging to hear how people have been drawn into the circle and made Jubilee their own. We owe so much to so many. Only a few are listed here: Dirk Jan Groot, Peter Benenson, Andrew Smith, Mike and Katie Morris, Brian Woods, Kate Blewett, Ian and Rosemary Andrews, Peter Fablan, John Whittington, John and Patsy Graham, Marlene Rice, Jim and Kitty Thompson, Bob Hitchings, James Parry, former MP Ian Bruce, Sam Yeghnazar, Ron George, Roger Forster, Simon Thomas, John Quanrud, Andy Lawrence, Gerald Coates, Alan Berry, Mike Wakely, Ian Matthews, Colin Collino and Bill Hampson.

Olivia Harrison's commitment was inspiring. Steve Brown never moved away.

Our fantastic supporters – as an organisation that is funded mostly by the generosity of our 'partners' – you're the best!

I don't know how to acknowledge my debt to people such as Father Shay Cullen, Petru Dugulescu, Valeri Barinov, Alexander Ogorodnikov, Timothy Chmykhalov, Rev K.K. Deveraj, Bob Fu, and so many others. You gave me so much and enriched my life beyond measure.

And thank you Shoba for letting me share your story. I'm so proud of you and grateful to God for all that you have accomplished.

Our friends who were just always there: George Verwer (who saved my life more than once), Sue Richards, Wanno Haneveld, Roley Horowitz, Dr Wai Sin Hu, Emma Foa and Reg Wright, Craig and Janet Rickards; my parents, Mum and Clement, for their abiding affection.

And to Joan, Jessica, Rachel and Luke: I love you.

Conclusion

Who Says You Can't Change the World?

Father Shay Cullen had taken me on a journey into a land that I never knew existed and from which there could be no return. Shay's epic struggle to bring sex criminals to justice had demonstrated that our anger and energy could find a practical expression to combat the structures of evil and bring real change for exploited and vulnerable children worldwide.

Around the planet, media pundits documented conflicts and warfare, directed by madmen, bandits, zealots, tyrants and terrorists, but hidden from view, moving invisibly but spreading fast, another conflict was being waged in this geography of disgrace: a war against children.

Tortured. Enslaved. Starved. Burnt. Maimed. Abused. Exploited. Prostituted. Brutalised. Forced to work. Compelled into violent conflicts. Murdered…

This is the terrifying experience of millions of children worldwide. Our global children, those most vulnerable and most in need of our care, are tragically, most at risk.

The campaign to change the law in Britain for sex offenders who commit their crimes overseas triumphed and demonstrated that ordinary people can make their voice heard for those whose voices have been silenced or forgotten or hidden. It showed that a campaign can be effective, using the media and the political system. When we raise prayer and action together we leave our personal footprint on the planet. We can make a difference.

That's the underlying – and overwhelming – message of Jubilee.

Beyond that, our hope is that Jubilee Campaign will continue to fulfil its mission: to be an instrument of justice.

If we follow in these footsteps, who says you can't change the world?

Jubilee Campaign is funded completely by our 'partners' – people who have entrusted us with their regular support each month. If you would like to become a partner or would like a free copy of *Just Right*, our human rights magazine published by Jubilee Action, write to:

Danny Smith
Jubilee
Cranleigh Road
Wonersh
Guildford
Surrey
GU5 0QX

danny@jubileecampaign.co.uk